CU00764511

Jonathan & Josie

Peb ninth by my calculation!

Brian Gilbart-Denham

invites you to assist him in launching his book

AROUND THE WORLD IN EIGHTY YEARS

(2 years short of his eighth decade!)

on Wednesday 2nd May 2012

at the Hurlingham Club (Quadrangle Room), London SW6 3PR

Parking available in club grounds

Drinks

6.30 - 8.30pm

No presents please

RSVP by 1st April 2012

20 Gladwyn Road, London SW15 1JY

briang-d@sky.com

———— Please bring this invitation with you to gain entry to the Hurlingham Club ————

AROUND THE WORLD IN 80 YEARS!

Or the

'official'

Life Of Brian

by

Brian Gilbart-Denham

*

Matador
9 Priory Business Park
Wistow Road
Kibworth Beauchamp
Leicestershire
LE8 0RX, UK
Tel: (+44) 116 279 2299
Email: books@troubador.co.uk
Web: www.troubador.co.uk/matador

ISBN 9781780882345

Matador is an imprint of Troubador Publishing Ltd.

Printed in Great Britain by the MPG Books Group, Bodmin and King's Lynn

For my family and friends

Out of chaos comes order *(Nietzsche).*
. . . luckily I had Mike George, a literarily-inclined friend and fellow-officer for whose persuasion, punctuation and paragraphing, encouragement and help I am most grateful. The flame of my resolve to complete this work was thereby ignited.

PROLOGUE

- *In the beginning* -

I MADE MY FIRST APPEARANCE IN THIS WORLD on Wednesday 2nd May 1934 - at number 20 Chester Square, Belgravia - London, SW1.

Concurrently, in Germany the Nazis were just starting their People's Court, while in neighbouring Austria a pact was being signed with the Vatican.

In the USSR Russia was joining the League of Nations and 'Uncle Joe' Stalin was planning his massacres.

China's leader, Mau Tse-Tung, was embarking on the Communists' Long March.

In England, Sir Oswald Moseley and his Black Shirts were put on trial.

Cats' Eyes and the trampoline were invented.

The UK population stood at 46-million.

George V was our reigning monarch, and the Loch Ness Monster had just been spotted for the first time, in Scotland.

Ramsay Macdonald was Prime Minister, and the same as Catherine the Great of Russia had done 200-years before, I emerged into the 1934 world on the second day of May that year - which was rather a different and more uncertain world than Catherine's had been in 1729.

My father, Vivian Vandeleur Gilbart-Denham, was a Lieutenant in the Irish Guards.

The best man at his wedding was his cousin, J.O.E. Vandeleur, who in World War Two went on to command the

1

Irish Guards Group of the Guards Armoured Division, in 1944, during the dash across the river Meuse-Escant Canal, and whose part was played by Michael Caine in the subsequent film *A Bridge Too Far.*

Joe told me once that on set the film's director, Sir Richard 'Dickie' Attenborough, insisted on calling him 'dahling'! - but Joe thought having Michael Caine play him in the part was fantastic.

My paternal grandfather was one Sir James Denham, the son of a Joseph Denham Smith, a celebrated evangelist, and Sarah Figgis Gilbart, the adopted daughter of James Gilbart FRS, the founder of Westminster Bank.

Chameleon-like, my grandfather was to change his name from Smith to Gilbart-Smith, then to Gilbart-Denham, and finally to Denham!

He was a poet, and also the author of *The Cradle of the Hapsburgs, The Log O' The Norseman* and *Serbelloni,* all of which works are still in print today.

Even as an undergraduate at Christ Church (Oxford) grandfather's gifts were apparent, fully recognised by his tutor, by Lewis Caroll, and later even by such men as Gladstone, Beaconsfield and Disraeli.

He married Grace Vandeleur, whose father was High Sheriff of County Clare.

The Vandeleurs were descended from a Dutch merchant, Maximillian Van de Leur, and had established their seat in Kilrush in 1687, where the family became influential during the 18th and 19th centuries.

My mother, Diana, on the other hand, came from a long line of Beaumonts, in Yorkshire.

One of her forbears, the seventeen-year-old Robert de Beaumont, had sailed with the Duke of Normandy (in 1066) with *'many knights from his family's manors'*, and was the first to follow the minstrel, Taifeller, in the assault of the Saxon stockade.

The Beaumonts were not good land owners, and one particular antecedent, Richard Beaumont, MA, FSA, JP –

known as 'The Antiquary of Whitley' (1748-1810) was apparently *a strange creature, half mad'*.

Someone else wrote about him: *'his home, which in its heyday - having been enlarged and modernised in part by James Paine - must have been a museum of treasure and beauty, was neglected.'* He gave away family pictures to the Bodleian and Ashmolean Museums, and a painting of the Beaumont family by Sir Joshua Reynolds was sold to the Tate Gallery.

The Beaumonts had been granted an estate in North Yorkshire, and this is where my maternal grandfather, Henry Beaumont, was born - at Whitley - in 1865.

Nine Beaumont girls had been born before my grandfather finally appeared, and such was everyone's joy at the arrival of this boy child that the babe was carried round the estate in celebratory stately fashion, borne aloft on a silver tray.

After leaving Eton and Cambridge he was commissioned into the King's Royal Rifle Corps (KRRC) and posted to Burma in the Chin Hills, in Lushai (India) and then to serve in the South African Cape during the Second Boer War, where he was present at the Relief of Ladysmith.

Whitley, the ancestral home, had been abandoned in 1906, and was demolished in 1952.

Grandfather retired from the Army in 1914, after having married Mary (May), the daughter of Sir James Gibson Craig of Ricarton, Edinburgh.

As a small boy I can remember him - Grandfather Henry Beaumont, with his long white beard - at his then home in Malton, Yorkshire, where his hunting trophies - lion, antelope, and tiger; panther, wildebeest and kudu, jackal and leopard adorned his garage walls.

ONE

- Childhood -

AT 11.00 A.M. ON SUNDAY 3rd SEPTEMBER 1939 Great Britain declared war against Adolf Hitler, and Germany.

A few weeks later my younger brother Seymour was born.

The two purely coincidental events were unrelated.

In anticipation of forthcoming developments – and here I mean the inevitability of WWII, not the impending birth of his third son - my father had left our Chester Square home in the summer of 1939 to join his Regiment, the Irish Guards.

Mother, still enceinte, then took my elder brother Desmond and me up to Yorkshire, there to join her sister, Bridget Goodhart, and her children, Joe and Diana, at Keldholme Priory - a former nunnery founded by Robert de Stuteville in the 13th century.

In the 14th century there were violent disputes and internal disorders at Keldholme Priory, and Archbishop Romanu directed the nuns to receive back one of their members, Christiana de Styvelington, who had apostatized, but having appeared before the chapter had 'manifested repentance', and desired to be allowed to return.

It was recorded that on one visit to Keldholme the Archbishop found that four of its nuns, one Isabella de Langetoft and three others, were 'incorrigible rebels'.

Prioresses were regularly dismissed from there.

In 1535 the royal commissioners themselves had occasion to visit Keldholme, and there were numbered then five nuns

4

besides the prioress, twelve servants and boys, and 'a piece of the true cross and a finger of St Stephen'.

Muriel Weber (a friend of my mother's) often used to stay at Keldholme. She was the seventh child of a seventh child, Scottish, and very psychic. She related later that she frequently saw habited nuns walking around the house.

I remember vividly the occasion I saw my governess dead at the bottom of the back stairs, down which she had tripped, fallen, and broken her neck. When a five-year-old I would often awaken terrified, hearing bumps and bangs in the night there, and would hurriedly pull the sheets up over my head.

For the next two years during term times I was sent to Hovingham Hall, to share lessons under Governess Brockie, with my six year old cousin, Katharine Worsley, whose home it was.

The Worsleys had bought the Manor of Hovingham in 1563.

They were an old Lancashire family, and legend would have it that they were descended from Elias, a giant who fought in the Crusades.

Katharine's father, Sir William Worsley, was President of the Yorkshire County Cricket Club, and captained Yorkshire in 1928 and 1929. I remember the cricket being played in front of the house, as it had been since 1858.

On one occasion Katharine and I performed a piano duet for the Women's Voluntary Service (WVS) in the Great Hall, with its many marble statues. Katharine did all the tricky little treble bits while I thumped out the base chords: it was a great success!

Then one day Aunt Joyce, Katharine's mother, summoned me to her study where she had the unpleasant task of giving me the sad news that my father had been wounded in battle, and had died. In those days children were brought up by their nannies and governesses, and only if well behaved would they appear before their parents, after tea. Because my father had been away soldiering so much around London, I had rarely ever seen him in any case, so I never really knew him.

Nevertheless, understandably I was to cry myself to sleep that night.

I remember that one day Aunt Joyce took Katharine and me up in the lift to see an aged woman lying in a four poster bed. She was Aunt Joyce's mother, who lay there sipping sieved prunes, because that was all the poor old lady was able to swallow.

Katharine Worseley, my six-year-old cousin, first girl friend and bedroom sharer, later went on to marry Prince Edward, who became the Duke of Kent.

On my eighth birthday, Saturday 2nd May 1942, accompanied by my elder brother Desmond, I went to Ludgrove Preparatory School, in Berkshire.

Ludgrove had just under 100 boys and was ruled with severity by its headmaster, Alan Barber, he who had captained the Yorkshire Cricket Team at the early age of 24.

At Ludgrove I was to learn Latin and algebra, cricket, soccer and scouting, and also how to bite my lip and not to cry when Barber beat me. I also learned how to suffer punishment 'drills' with heavy WW1 rifles, under Sergeant Major Goldie, as well as how to box and fence.

During German air raids (this was the third year of WWII, remember) we would troop down to the underground bunkers where we spent the rest of the night.

Among my contemporaries at Ludgrove were Colin Ingleby-Mackenzie, the undisputed winner of every coveted school sports award; Alexander Thynne (our head boy), Charles Douglas Home, whose bother Robin said to me: 'My young brother will be in your dormitory; he's a clever little sod, look after him!'

There was also a chap called Paul Foot - and my cousin Katharine's future husband, Edward Kent, who was regularly thrashed by Barber, the head.

It was definitely sport rather than academics that was the lodestar at Ludgrove.

Officers 1st Bn The Irish Guards – Presentation of Colours 1927: my father, rear row far left

My mother, Diana, with big brother Desmond, baby Seymour, and self

Eton College Fencing Team – 1952:
Back Row R. Harman; L. Laxton
Front Row S. Mackay; Author; P. Wilmot-Sitwell

Sgt. F. Colley's   Brigade Squad.
GUARDS DEPOT   FEBRUARY. 1955.

Gdsn. T. MacNeece, R. Gilbert-Denham, G. Shipman, Sgt. W. Brown, Gdsn. N. Cobbold, P. Cobbold, T. Brassey.
(P.T. Instr.)
Gdsn. D. Davenport, P. Bottam, A. Grant, P. Porter, T. Craig, P. Gibbs, T. Pugh, A. Dunran, The Hon. J. Morrion, Tpr. Lord Thynne.
Gdsn. The Hon R. Ingham, Sgt. W. Fox, SGT. F. COLLEY, Capt. The Hon. E. H. K Digby, T.d.S. Bell, Sgt. L. Hart, Gdsn. J. Morrogh Bernard.
(W.T Instr)   Squad Instr   (Asstnt Sgt)

Gdsn. A. Corbill,   P. Grant.

10

When Desmond and I were at home on holiday in Yorkshire, German aircraft used to fly over our Kirbymoorside area on bombing raids to York and Leeds. They would release their bombs at random, and in order to distract our radar would also drop streamers of silver paper, which we used to enjoy collecting. Desmond and I, out on our bikes, had become quite good at distinguishing the different drone sounds of Allied and German aircraft, and if ever we heard enemy planes above we would instinctively dive into a ditch.

I remember one bomb landed just the other side of the River Dove, and blew out many Keldholme windows.

On another occasion, returning from Hovingham one day, I found that the photographs of my father in the drawing room had been removed, to become replaced by pictures of a gentleman called Gerald Kildare, to whom my mother had now become engaged. Besides being a Marquess, I thought Gerald was a really nice man . . . but as for Mother removing Father's photograph . . . well . . . *La donna e mobile!* - but like many wartime romances theirs, too, failed to blossom or flower to full fruition.

TWO

- *Eton* - *& my teen years* -

ETON COLLEGE WAS FOUNDED by Henry V1 in 1440.

In 1687 it had 207 boys, but when I went there in 1948 there were over 1000 of us, in 26 houses and with 160 teaching staff.

The taller boys wore tails coats and the shorter boys bum jackets, all in black, in memory of King George the Third.

I joined E.P. Hedley's house, opposite the *Burning Bush.*

This was just three years after the end of WWII and one year after the great 'freeze' of 1947 when the whole country was snowed-in for months and temperatures dropped to minus 21 degrees. With the spring thaw came the worst floods for 250 years, and then the warmest summer since 1659. The post-war nation was suffering fuel shortages, food rationing (only 43gs of cheese and 4oz chocolate a week, for example) and not only were things like bananas, avocado pears or mangos unseen – they were almost unheard of.

Housemaster Hedley was a kind and considerate beak, and soon after I left he was to take holy orders, but whether there was any connection I'm not sure. He went on to become the vicar of Wargrave.

Each House had a 'Dame' who would administer treatment for coughs and minor injuries sustained in our field games, such as Eton's renowned Wall Game, Fives, or any of our many other sporting pursuits.

On one occasion my Dame was treating an outbreak of adolescent spots that had erupted on my back, when - for some reason that I no longer recall - in walked none other than the great actor, Lawrence Olivier, whose son, Tarquin, was a boy in the house.

Senior boys had junior boys assigned to them to light their coal fires, make their toast for tea and all manner of other tasks. They would yell '*Boy Up*' whenever they wanted to dispatch a message somewhere within the school.

The house captain, who was judge and jury, was allowed to flog boys at his own discretion.

We swam naked in the Thames, the Lower Boys in one stretch of the water and the Upper Boys in another, but then these Thames swims ceased when a number of boys, Princess Margaret's husband Tony Armstrong Jones being one of them, contracted polio.

In 1637 the East India Company's Francis Day, the founding father of Madras (Chennai) and one of the first Englishman to survive a stinking hot Madras summer, ascribed his survival to '*conditioning to a tough life by my schooling at Eton, and jumping naked into the freezing Thames in winter*'.

I 'messed' with two very good mates, Gavin Reed and Simon Smail.

Our drawing master was Wilfred Blunt, brother of the notorious traitor.

My German tutor was A.J. Marsden, a nephew of Eton's infamous earlier maths master, H.K. 'Bloody Bill' Marsden.

As an expert linguist, John Marsden had been given an intelligence role in WWII, and took part in the commando raid on the Lofoten Islands off Norway, when a German ship was captured containing codes which played a crucial role in solving the Ultra secret. Later, he was parachuted into Africa, where he worked behind Italian lines.

Promoted to lieutenant-colonel, he commanded an independent unit working with Eisenhower's staff for the D-Day invasion, a role which involved his training and qualifying as a pilot. Finally, in the immediate aftermath of the war, he was on the staff of the Control Commission in Germany – at one point being instrumental in dismissing the Bürgermeister of Cologne, one Konrad Adenauer, for 'insubordination', which allowed Adenauer to go forth and campaign for office on the slogan: 'Sought after by the Russians, imprisoned by the Nazis, sacked by the British.'

A soldier whose turnout and discipline were commended personally by Montgomery, Marsden was mentioned in dispatches, and was awarded the Croix de Guerre with Palms by France's General Charles de Gaulle, and the American Bronze Star by Eisenhower. The rumour at Eton was that his intelligence role had been an unusually active one, and that he was the inspiration for Geoffrey Household's thriller *Rogue Male*, about a plot to assassinate Hitler. John died in 2004, at the age of 88.

Those of us in the Combined Cadet Force (CCF) trained hard, and in 1952 had the honour of street lining for George VI's funeral when the King's body was brought to Windsor by the steam engine *'Windsor Castle'* before being interred at St George's Chapel.

My time at Eton was enjoyable, and not especially distinguished – apart, that is, from becoming Captain of Fencing.

THREE

- *Joining the Army* -

IN 1877 THE LAND adjoining the North Downs' Surrey village of Caterham's Metropolitan Asylum (which had opened in October 1870 to house 2,000 unfortunate inmates) was transformed into the Guards Depot.

These new barracks were a prime example of barrack reform following the Crimean War of 1853-6, when soldiers were kept in *'condition of overcrowding and squalor as bad as workhouses or prisons'.*

But it was still a pretty grim place for us new recruits to go to, in February 1953!

There were 20 of us in St Colley's Brigade Squad, all having been designated as potential officers, with the Hon. E. Digby our Commanding Officer and Guardsman Bell our trained soldier.

Basic military training lasted 13 weeks, with inspections every 4 weeks.

Failing drill or a weapon inspection meant a week's back squadding.

'Shining parade' took place from 6 - 9.30 every evening, with one of us assigned to go to the NAAFI to buy food.

We 'bulled' up our boots to shine like mirrors, ironed the creases of our battle dress trousers, and learnt Regimental history, and all about battle honours and traditions.

Braces, groundsheets, puttees and clothing, eating utensils, mess tins and equipment – all of these items of kit, and more, had to be laid out on our beds with minute precision to undergo the scrutiny of regular kit inspections.

One of our number, Andrew Duncan, turned up late to join the squad - from Canada.

He arrived immaculately dressed, with bowler hat and umbrella.

'Squad – *Squad* . . . Atten-SHUN' screamed Trained Soldier Bell, understandably having mistaken Andrew for an officer.

Thirty-seconds later, swiftly divested of his finery and wearing his freshly issued denims Recruit Duncan was to find himself furiously engaged in polishing the bubbles out of his crinkly new pair of boots.

For us public school boys it was probably the first time we had mixed with working class lads. Most of us were physically immature compared with the recruits from the mines and industries in Belfast, Cardiff and Glasgow.

Having sat the Civil Service written examination at Eton, and passed, and then got through the Army's Regular Commissions Board (RCB) tests at Westbury, I was eligible to join the Royal Military College at Sandhurst for two years, as a Gentleman Cadet.

Sandhurst was an imposing building that had been purchased by William Pitt the Younger from some poor relatives of his in 1812, for the then sum of £2,600.

In 1862 there was mutiny over food, and the year 1929 saw the first arrival of Moslem and Hindu cadets from India – but of course the history of Sandhurst is slightly wider reaching than just these two snippets I came across and relate here!

When I arrived there, in 1952, Jack Lord was the College RSM. He became famous (along with many other reasons) for addressing cadets drawn up on their first parade with his traditional introduction: 'Gentlemen, when you speak to me you will call me *'Sir'* and when I speak to you, I, in return, shall call *you* 'Sir'. The only *difference* is that IN YOUR CASE *YOU WILL MEAN IT!'*

I was to share a room with Andrew Duncan, our sartorially elegant late arrival recruit, whom I had earlier met at the Guards Depot, in Caterham.

A former soldier was allocated to us as our batman, and he cleaned and polished our boots and Sam Browne belts.

Up until 1870 army commissions and promotions used to be purchased, and now here *we* were being *paid* to acquire ours!

For the next two years we were to study military history, languages, and accounting; military law, vehicle mechanics, how to ride a motorbike, oh - and how to command a division – in my case an arguably unnecessary skill, when upon commissioning I discovered that in the first instance I was only to be entrusted with commanding a platoon of 30 Irish soldiers.

We competed with each other crossing over horrendous assault courses, on the drill square under various bawling CSMs, and from time to time the even more fearsome RSM Jackie Lord himself, of course.

And we were consistently being 'examined' – not medically, but in the classroom.

On a couple of occasions a fellow cadet, Tom McNiece, took me out to have tea with a relative of his, one Field Marshal Bernard Law Montgomery, the Viscount Alamein, so enobled after one of his most famous WWII battles, against the German Field Marshal Erwin 'The Desert Fox' Rommel's Afrika Korps in the North African desert, which proved to be one of the most crucial turning points of the war for the British.

Monty delighted in telling me how when he'd been a cadet himself at Sandhurst, he had once set fire to a colleague's shirt tail, and also how much he had disliked his cadet training, but he stated that he believed emphatically in the need for an 'Ecôle Militaire'.

Taking us outside at his home in Alton Mill in Hampshire, he proudly showed us his desert caravan 'home' with its framed photograph of his arch-rival, Rommel, on one of its panels - and went on to further recount tales of his battles at El Alamein.

Before our great Passing Out Parade ceremony, I managed to lead the Sandhurst fencing team with impressive wins over Cranwell and Dartmouth in the Royal Tournament, and also to win the Cadet Inter Services Foil Championship.

FOUR

– Soldiering in Egypt –

IN 1875 GREAT BRITAIN'S PRIME MINISTER, Mr Benjamin Disraeli, purchased the Khedive of Egypt's 40 per cent shares in the Suez Canal, which had been designed by Ferdinand de Lesseps and constructed by the French six years previously.

This act made Britain the biggest Suez shareholder.

Sailing times between London and Bombay were now cut dramatically.

In 1922 and 1936 Anglo-Egyptian treaties were signed allowing British troops to remain in and guard the Canal Zone, where they had been stationed since 1882.

In 1951 the Egyptian Government declared the 1936 agreement void, abrogated it, and arranged for its police, troops and terrorist *Fedayeen* to start harassing British troops and their families.

To combat these terrorist attacks on British camps, with all the sniping, abductions, murder and sabotage, the garrison in the Zone had to be increased to 80,000 personnel.

It was to this scenario of heightened military threat that I arrived as a young subaltern in 1954, to join my regiment, the Irish Guards, stationed in Fanara, near Fayid.

Funnily enough, this was to be my second tour in Egypt!

I had first been there at the age of two, when my father was stationed in Kasr el Nil barracks, in 1936. April of that year saw the appointment of 'His Majesty Farouk 1, by the grace of God, King of Egypt and Sudan, Sovereign of Nubia, of Kordofan, and of Darfur'. Farouk had an Albanian father and Egyptian mother and had been educated at the Royal Military Academy, Woolwich. Aged two, I didn't attend his coronation, but initially the 16-year-old King was hugely popular. In one radio broadcast he told his people '. . . I am prepared for all sacrifices in the cause of my duty'. Soon afterwards he acquired dozens of palaces, hundreds of cars, a lust for travel to Europe on grand shopping sprees, and a huge collection of pornography. After having an enormous dinner in the *Ile de France* restaurant in Rome one night in 1965, he was to die, aged 45 - 'a stomach with a head' - weighing 21 stone.

In 1954, however, our camp consisted of hundreds of 120 lb tents, and even by 7 o'clock each morning the canvas of these tents would already be scalding hot from the sun.

Lavatories consisted of deep trench latrines, and when on one occasion one of them collapsed, our commanding officer, Savill Young, with memorable ignominiousness, fell into it.

Having learnt to command a division at Sandhurst, I found one of my typical platoon responsibilities in Egypt - foot inspections – relatively unexciting. I wrote to my grandmother about the boredom I felt, telling her that the only two books in our company office were the Manual of Military Law and the Bible. With immediate hindsight I realized that perhaps I should not have done this, and was proved right, because soon afterwards I started to receive regular postings from Granny about 'Searching the Scriptures'.

I always looked forward to cucumber and banana sandwiches at tea in the officers' mess: and especially listening to Captain Arthur Moore, son of the Queen's horse trainer, and a great Irish raconteur, who kept his audience of young officers spellbound for hours, till all the tables had been cleared and the staff had disappeared.

My platoon was often called upon to provide patrols and guards for 10 Base Ordnance Depot, a vast collection of stores left over from WWII. Despite all our deterrent mines and barbed wire, the Egyptians were skilful at penetrating the Ordnance hangers and stealing anything they could find, from water bottles to armoured cars.

Our guardsmen, who had little or no education, were required to attend classes in the afternoons to learn reading and writing.

My abiding memories of Egypt are many and varied, principal perhaps being our desert manoeuvres when one litre of water per man had to last five hours in temperatures of 100F. (Water discipline was de rigueur and doctors and generals at that time did not know that in that climate the human body requires at least 2 quarts of water each hour).

The destitution seen in local Egyptian villages was also unpleasantly memorable, as were the lack of compassion and total indifference to poverty shown by the occupying troops. Today's officers would undergo initial language training in order to be able to converse with the population; platoons would carry out 'hearts and minds' campaigns, and engineers would drill water holes.

One of my regrets is that, during my monotonous duties in MELF 27 (Middle East Land Forces) I did not appreciate that these very Egyptians we disparaged so much, had begun to write their hieroglyphic signs about 3,300 BC, and our camps stood on land that even before the Pharaohs had raised their prodigious edifices along the Nile, was the world's second great civilisation.

Other than swimming, and the occasional visit to Cairo, along with most of my peers I found life in the Canal Zone extremely tedious, and so one day I volunteered for a posting to Kenya, a much more exciting place, where there was a war going on against the Mau Mau.

FIVE

– Kenya, & fighting the Mau Mau –

FOR SEVERAL DECADES IN EAST AFRICA the grabbing of Kikuyu land in the central highlands of Kenya by European settlers had become an increasingly bitter pill of contention.

European colonisers allowed about 120,000 Kikuyu to farm patches of land in exchange for their labour.

The resultant inevitable upsurge of Kikuyu unrest and civil disobedience led to the formation and emergence of mindlessly vicious Mau Mau thugs, who held barbaric oath rituals, before going on to burn down European residences, butcher the owners with machetes and hamstring their livestock.

The average Mau Mau band was about 100 strong.

In the Aberdare forest they were led by Dedan Kimathi, and in Mount Kenya by a man called Waruhiu Itote (known as General China).

Attacking isolated farms and suburbs around Nairobi, they killed 1,800 loyal African Christians, landowners and opponents.

In 1952 Kenya's newly arrived Governor, Sir Evelyn Baring, declared a state of emergency, as a consequence of which 8,000 people were arrested.

The GOC-in-Chief, East Africa Command, General Sir George Erskine, declared the Aberdares and Mount Kenya to be 'Prohibited Areas'.

I sailed down the Red Sea to Mombasa in a troop ship, playing bridge with Lt Colonel Duncan Vaughan who had just been appointed to command his battalion, the King's Shropshire Light Infantry (KSLI) in Kenya.

Soon after arriving, he was shot dead whilst out in the bush inspecting one of his own ambushes.

Unlike my own regiment, the Irish Guards, who considered any newly joined officer as some sort of virus to be avoided, the officers' mess of the 23rd Battalion King's African Rifles were a hospitable bunch who warmly welcomed everyone, and it was to them that I was to be attached.

Andrew Hlwati, our Polish second in command, insisted on lending me his powerful wartime Beretta revolver, and with this impliment strapped to my hip I was soon whisked away deep into the Aberdares to join my heterogeneous platoon of Kamba and Kikuyu, Meru and Luo, and Masai and Turkana askaris, all of whom were principally distinguishable by their tribal scars and pierced ears.

Gradually I picked up Swahili, and learned to sing *Moja mbili na quenda, quenda kalima shamba* - One man went to mow, went to mow a meadow.

We had large radios, but reception was usually difficult.

The Africans used their inherent rhythmic skills to communicate in Morse code at an incredible speed.

We tracked the Mau Mau every day, following leads of broken twigs, footprints, porcupine quills (often used by them as signs) and smoke from their terrorist fires.

Our principal quarry was the 35-year-old leader, Dedan Kimathi.

On Mount Kenya our task was to patrol the long ditch fortified with panjis *(*sharpened bamboo sticks) that had been constructed to stop the Mau Mau crossing from the forest into the villages for food.

If any Mau Mau did appear in the villages the bibi (women) would emit ululating cries to alert our patrols, their eerie wailing being heard for miles.

Sometimes the RAF would bomb suspected terrorist hideouts in the forest, and this terrified the animals. Once my patrol was charged down the game track by a family of screaming rhino. One of my askari, not quite quick enough to scale a tree, was gored, making his fellow askaris hoot with laughter at his plight.

My eight months secondment to 23 KAR was a memorable and happy experience. I admired and respected my askaris, and was sad to return to Egypt.

On Mt Kenya our task was to patrol the long ditch fortified with panjis (sharpened bamboo sticks) to deter bands of Mau Mau

Moscow's Red Square; May Day 1957 . . . a four hours parade of tanks, guns, workers and school children, with the author and friend Peter Thomas participating as well . .

My anti-tank platoon outside St Hilarion's Castle, Cyprus - 1958

A force of some 50 army cadets wearing Afrika Korps caps and swastikas loudly *heiled* Hitler and prepared to sell their lives dearly to prevent the kidnapping of Venus . . . .

SIX

– A short Russian interlude –

STATIONED IN SHORNCLIFFE, KENT, in 1957, my brother officer Peter Thomas and I decided we would drive to Moscow.

The Cold War was in full swing.

Nikita Kruschev, who had taken over from Joseph Stalin in 1953, was fearfully renowned for his draconian dealing with the Hungarian uprising that had erupted in 1956.

In the USA Senator Joe McCarthy was looking for reds under the beds, and at the same time Americans were engaged in a war in Vietnam, in which 58,000 of their servicemen would eventually die.

It was against this backdrop of global activity that Peter and I planned to drive my Volkswagen through Berlin, Brest Litovsk, Posnan, Warsaw and Minsk, and then Smolensk, to arrive in Moscow by 1st May to see the famous Russian May Day Parade. On reaching Berlin we were to find ourselves peremptorily being marched in to see the Head of the British Military Mission to Russian Forces, the Russian-speaking General Miles Fitzalan-Howard, 17th Duke of Norfolk – a fellow Guardsman. 'The Micks are drama, and you two are no exception,' stormed General Miles, a Grenadier. 'You have the Government of East Germany stamped on your passports, and we do not *rec*ognize the Government of East Germany. Anyway -,' he said, his tone softening, 'I wish you well.' Then with a wink and a broad smile, his official rant over, he shook our hands, and sent us on our way.

In April 1812 Napoleon's Grande Armée of 449,000 men, 6,000 supply wagons and 1,146 cannon had also set out for the same destination!

Short of Smolensk, on 7th September 1812, they attacked the Imperial Russian Army of General Mikhail Kutuzov near the village of Borodino, west of the town of Mozhaysk, and eventually captured the main positions on the battlefield, but failed to destroy the Russian army, and so lost the battle. It was the largest and bloodiest single-day action of the French invasion of Russia, involving more than 250,000 troops and resulting in at least 70,000 casualties. About a third of Napoleon's soldiers were killed or wounded, but other contributory factors to their defeat were thunderstorms, wagons sinking up to their hubs, horses dropping from exhaustion, men losing their boots, starvation, desertion, typhoid and suicide . . .

. . . my friend Peter and I hoped to do better.

Before departure we had a meeting with an MI6 officer to discuss and 'clear' our proposed trip with him, and were told that we should ignore any warnings that might be given to us by the Russian authorities about 'unpassable roads'.

'Westerners are not allowed to drive in that part of Russia,' said an MI6 man, 'because they don't want to risk us taking photos. But don't be put off!'

And so we departed.

After motoring for days through the cobbled roads of Poland, we arrived at the Russian Polish border, at Brest Litovsk, where we met our Russian guide. He took us into an office where we were advised by a senior official to put our car on a goods wagon, because the road from there to Minsk was flooded, and so after 'some persuasion' we agreed to his suggestion.

For many miles the countryside on both sides of the railway embankment was submerged, and travelling by train felt more like sailing – but eventually we reached Moscow.

Red Square.

The May Day Parade.

1957.

Four 'Bison' bombers escorted by Mig-17 jet fighters flew overhead, whilst on the ground a Hero of the Soviet Union by the name of Birykov led a breathtakingly impressive four-hour parade of tanks, guns, workers and school children – at which Peter and I were promptly moved to grab two bunches of flowers, and join in.

We also joined the tourist queue at Lenin's tomb and saw his waxen face gazing up at us.

Was it really happening?

I had received an introduction to Sir D'Arcy Patrick Reilly, Great Britain's new Ambassador to Moscow, and soon we found ourselves invited to lunch by this courteous gentleman - quite a smart affair, with Russian waiters in tail coats and white ties.

I asked Sir Patrick how he ever managed to engage safely in private conversations, in the oppressive and monitored Soviet environment, to which he replied: 'We found 32 'bugs' in our last anti-bug drive, and so when we want to talk confidentially we go out into the garden, or else into the loo, and then pull the chain!'

Peter, the Volkswagen and I completed our 3,000 mile car and rail journey exhilarated and unscathed, having fared a great deal better than Napoleon's wretched troops had done.

SEVEN

- Cyprus -

Ethnikí Orgánosis Kipriakoú Agónos (or EOKA – Greek for National Organisation of Cypriot Struggle) was a Greek Nationalist military resistance organisation that fought for the end of British rule of Cyprus, as well as for self-determination and for union with Greece (Enosis).

It all began in 1955, with ambushes, assassinations and the bombing of a series of targets throughout the island.

EOKA, whose aim was '*The liberation of Cyprus from the British yoke*' was headed by Colonel George Grivas, who had served in the Greek army in both world wars. He was supported and encouraged in his endeavours by the Greek Cypriot Archbishop Michail Makarios III.

In 1958 Sir Hugh ('Pussy') Foot replaced Field Marshal Sir John Harding as the last Governor of Cyprus (the island was granted independence in 1960), and Major General Kendrew was appointed Director of Operations.

The Turkish-Cypriot community was whipped into a frenzy by broadcasts from Turkey calling for partition of the island, and this resulted in the birth of the Turkish Resistance Organisation (TMT).

While walking his two-year-old son along Nicosia's Ledra Street - soon to become known as 'Murder Mile' - a British army soldier, Sergeant Hammond, was shot dead.

The Army arrested a hundred Cypriots and took them to detention centres.

Communal violence broke out with the massacre of eight Greeks in a Turkish cornfield.

40,000 British troops were attempting to combat EOKA and keep the peace between the warring communities.

Then into this historic island, colonised and developed down the years by Romans, Greeks and Crusaders, Lusignans, Venetians and Turks - and the British - there arrived in the summer of 1958 . . . 1st Battalion Irish Guards.

After a hot and dusty start in Nicosia employed on cordon and search operations, the battalion moved north to Kyrenia, where the hills were dominated by that most incredible example of Middle Ages architecture, St Hilarion Castle, which had certainly been standing when King Richard and his Crusaders conquered the island in 1191.

We patrolled by day and night, following leads which invariably led to monasteries where arms were stored but where we were forbidden to enter.

At dusk and night the Greeks used kite-borne lamps to warn their people of military patrols.

Barking 'pi' dogs proved a menace.

I recall my anti-tank platoon being introduced to a new 106mm weapon by our neighbouring parachute battalion - not that we were using anti-tank weapons against EOKA!

We guarded the enormous Kikomo Trimithea (KT) detention camp with its corridors of barbed wire and grinning bearded Greek detainees.

A number of Greek fighters were hanged.

We used to lunch at the Ledra Palace Hotel, the haunt and habitat of the Press.

My younger brother Seymour was also in Cyprus at the same time as me, serving as a trooper with the Royal Horse Guards, having a hairy time of it patrolling in his armoured 'Ferret' scout car.

I took the opportunity to write to Seymour's squadron leader, Johnny Watson, a formidable contributor to *The Field* and *Horse and Hound*, asking whether he might be good enough to consider recommending that Seymour be given another crack at a commissioning interview.

In declining my request his reply stated that he did not really consider Seymour to be proper 'officer material'.

Later - Lt Col Sir Seymour Gilbart-Denham, KCVO, CVO, Crown Equerry, was to prove Major Watson's prognosis slightly misjudged.

After Cyprus I was posted to the Guards Depot at Pirbright, training recruits. Whilst there I decided to take the opportunity to learn to fly during my off-duty hours, at White Waltham airfield, near Maidenhead, where my instructor introduced me to an American 2-seater Aircoup A-2A, described in *Life Magazine* as being 'nearly foolproof'.

For weeks I practiced 'circuits and bumps', taking off and landing on the airstrip, and getting myself out of a spin when spiralling earthward. Before it was time for me to go solo and gain my PPL (Provisional Pilot's Licence) however, I received warning of a pending overseas posting, thus precluding any further skylarking - fate's intervention thereby probably saving the lives of both myself and the Aircoup A-2A.

EIGHT

- Cowboys & Goatherds -

IN 1951 HODDER & STOUGHTON published a book by the author Jerrard Tickell, called *Appointment with Venus* - about the kidnapping of a cow!

The story's synopsis is that in 1940, after the fall of France, the fictitious Channel Island of Armorel is occupied by a small garrison of German troops under the benign command of a Hauptmann Weiss. He finds that the hereditary ruler, the Suzerain, is away in the army, leaving the Provost in charge.

Back in London, the Ministry of Agriculture realises that Venus, a valuable pedigree Guernsey cow, remains on the island. They petition the War Office to mount a rescue operation, and Major Valentine Morland is assigned the mission, with the assistance of the Suzerain's sister, Nicola Fallaize, who had joined the ATS at the outbreak of war.

They travel to Armorel by submarine, contact the Provost and other friends on the island, and discover that Weiss, a cattle breeder in civilian life, is about to have the cow shipped to Germany. By a series of elaborate deceptions, they then manage to extract Venus from Weiss's command and succeed in returning her to England.

The book was successfully filmed in 1951, starring David Niven, Glynis Johns and Kenneth More.

Back in England, strange unusual duties for an army officer sometimes unveil.

One such of these was when I found myself posted to take part in a cadet leadership course at Thetford, Norfolk, in 1959.

Quite by coincidence, one of the participating cadets at this event was Savill Young, from Harrow School, the son of our regimental colonel.

A Coldstream Guards officer, glorying in the name of Torquil Matheson, devised a wonderfully imaginative exercise to test the cadets' initiative etc.

The best way I can describe what it was all about is to quote the author, Jerrard Tickell's, own words, when he 'got wind of' what was happening, and attended.

Last night *(Tickell wrote)* on an imaginary island in the middle of Norfolk, over a hundred young warriors from the Combined Cadet Forces of schools in Eastern Command had an appointment with a Venus who had changed her shape, sex and species, in order to provide them with a three-day exercise re-enacting my original Venus rescue story.

A force of some 50 cadets wearing swastikas on their Afrika Korps caps, loudly *heiled* Hitler and prepared to sell their lives dearly to prevent the kidnapping of Venus.

An imaginery salty ocean gushed and surged beyond the perimeter tapes . . . bren-gun blanks banged, thunder-flashes exploded, and much acrid smoke drifted across the 'island'.

I ran Venus to ground in the kitchen of a ruined house, where I found 'him' contentedly munching a bunch of cigarettes.

He consented to give me an exclusive interview.

I asked 'Venus' (a billy-goat) how he liked being a stand-in for a pedigree Guernsey cow.

'My *own* pedigree' he retorted, with something of a haughty snort, 'I'll have you know, is as long as that of any Guernsey cow. I had hoped to be led up the garden path by Glynis Johns, but you can't have everything.

'Got any cigarettes, by the way?'

Some years later a young man stopped me (the author – not Jerrard Tickell) in Peter Jones. 'Excuse me,' he said, 'I believe I recognize you as my Platoon Commander on a Cadet Leadership Course we had in Thetford a few years ago. You might like to know that I am now a clergyman.'

NINE

- *Down Under* -

'I WILL TEACH YOU HOW TO BOIL AN EGG FIRST', my mother said, on learning that I was to be posted out to Australia and would be living in a self-catering apartment.

Her lesson proved to be invaluable!

Many people naturally think and assume it is Sydney, but it is Canberra that has been the nation's capital city - since 1910.

I was going there to join the United Kingdom Joint Services Liaison Staff (UKJSLS), to where the British High Commission had recently moved.

By 1961 the National University and most of the Embassies had relocated themselves from Melbourne to Canberra.

Canberra took its name from Ngambri, a rendition of the name of the aboriginal people of the area.

The Royal Military College, Duntroon, situated in the former Campbell estates in Canberra, was named from Campbell's Duntrune Castle, in Argyll.

UKJSLS was situated in the Department of Defence.

The head of UKJSLS was Major General Joe Kendrew, DSO and three bars.

One of my jobs was to look after the interests of British Army personnel, including those ADCs who were stationed all over Australia.

My tour did not start well.

Within just a few days of arrival I was marched in before the furious British High Commissioner, Sir William Oliver, for flouting the High Commission's very strict rules about the importation of foreign cars.

I had had the temerity to bring out a 2.4 litre Jaguar for use in Canberra, *and* a Volkwagen to drive on dirt roads.

Sir William strictly forbade me use of the VW in Canberra, and placed me on probation for three months – but then the following evening invited me to dinner!

Canberra was wonderfully situated for skiing, in Thredbo and Perisha in the winter months, and for surfing around Sydney in the summer.

Being a reasonable skier I was given a red cross shirt and a free ski pass, in return for helping those who had come to grief on the slush and grass on the lower slopes.

My duties in UKJSLS included escorting visiting British VIPs to the Hydro Electric plants in the Snowy Mountains, and talking to audiences of the Returned Servicemen's League (RSL).

I flew across to Papua, New Guinea, engaged in redeploying the Pacific Islands Regiment (PIR) personnel in Port Moresby, Wewak, Lae, and Mt Hagen, often being greeted on these visits by tribesmen with spears, penis-gourds and exotic feathered headdress.

I was very wary of these tribesmen.

In 1895 the Rev James Chalmers had observed the people of the Purari Delta, one of whom admitted to this Christian gentleman:

'I killed one wife, and Iomu the other. I killed the woman with a dagger of cassowary bone. We took the bodies in the canoe and took them back with us. I did not bite off the woman's nose. It is not our custom to bite off the nose of a person you have killed. If I kill a man or a woman, someone else bites off the nose.'

When the Doboduras capture an enemy,' the Rev Chalmers reported, 'they slowly torture him to death, practically eating him alive. When he is almost dead, they make a hole in the side of his head and scoop out his brains with a kind of wooden spoon. These brains, which are often warm and fresh, are regarded as a great delicacy.'

A fellow Mick, Lt Col Bill Crowther, was the comptroller at Government House, and he often invited me to formal dinner parties with the Governor General Viscount de L'Isle, who in 1943 had won a VC in defence of the Anzio beachhead.

Bill Crowther - a stickler for protocol - confided in me after one dinner that he had been extremely frustrated when the famous conductor, Sir Malcolm Sergeant, had declined to bow to the Governor General.

I enjoyed these dinners immensely, especially eating on solid gold plates from the family home at Penshurst.

Major General Geordie Gordon Lennox and his wife Nan once arrived in Canberra. I was appointed to be his ADC when he went on an official visit to Duntroon Military College, with its four companies representing Australia's war past: Gallipoli (Turkey), Alamein, (Egypt), Kokoda (Papua New Guinea) and Kapyong (South Korea) – but it was Nan who was very much 'the Inspecting Officer!'

With the plethora of visitors we had I was able to establish relationships which took me to embassies and headquarters in Indonesia, Singapore and New Zealand, and spent some enjoyable days with Douglas Montagu Douglas Scott, in Adelaide. Douglas, a Mick, was ADC to Air Vice Marshal Sir Robert George, and married his daughter.

When I left Australia, in 1962, huge digging machines were preparing to transform Canberra into a lake city, with the construction of Lake Burley Griffin.

TEN

– Deutschland – & BAOR –

THE 1945 POTSDAM CONFERENCE divided Germany into four separate occupation zones, controlled by the French in the South-West, by the British in the North-West, by the United States in the South – and by the USSR in the East.

Great Britain drew the short straw, and got the rainy industrial Ruhr.

Berlin, too, was also divided into four sectors, controlled by the four super powers.

The year 1942 had seen five months of strategic Allied bombing of the Ruhr, with its Krupp armaments in Essen and Rheinmetal-Bersig plant in Düsseldorf.

On 30 May the RAF with 868 aircraft dropped 1445 tons of bombs, and in Cologne alone destroyed seven banks, nine hospitals, 17 churches, 16 schools, four universities and four hotels.

150,000 fled the city.

After the war the Soviets sent 165,000 Poles and Czechs to Siberia, the US started the Marshal Plan, the Allies stationed troops for NATO defence, and under their president, Dr Konrad Adenauer, Western Germany experienced an 'economic miracle' with two decades of unprecedented growth.

In 1961, to stop the flow of refugees to the West, East Germany constructed the notorious Berlin Wall.

It was in 1962 that I arrived in this backdrop of German prosperity and threat of nuclear war, to join my battalion in Hubbelrath, on the outskirts of Dusseldorf.

With the shortage of married quarters, our commanding officer, Stephen Langton, had acquired a number of mobile homes that were parked on the barracks square.

Our lives alternated between training, large scale exercises, caring for married families and keeping our soldiers out of the local urban bars and brothels.

Back home in London the War Minister, John Profumo, angrily crossed swords with Labour's Emanuel Shinwell over some embarrassing behaviour in Germany, of the Cameronians (Poisoned Dwarfs).

In Hamburg's Kaiserkeller the Beatles were fired when George Harrison tacked a condom to the wall of the nightclub. Soon afterwards, when Beatle hysteria took over the world, the Beatles were to perform in front of the Queen and Prince Philip, inviting the audience to 'clap your hands . . . or rattle your jewellery, as appropriate!'

Land owners in Schleswig Holstein reaped a rich financial harvest when our battalions of 'Pig' one-ton armoured troop-carrying Humbers and squadrons of tanks advanced over their countryside engaged in mock battles. Farmers would follow the vehicles with notebook and pencil in hand, recording damaged fences, injured livestock and the number of squashed turnips, and present their bills for compensation to the military authorities.

Schleswig Holstein was full of grand houses: we were billeted in one of them, where our company commander, David Faulkner, entertained us with renditions of Liszt and Chopin on the resident Steinway.

About half our soldiers were National Servicemen, whose pay was a mere 28 shillings a week, as against the British average man's then earning of £15.10.

Since 1945 there had been well over two million National Service conscripts, 400 of whom lost their lives in Korea and Malaya.

The last National Serviceman was to leave the army in 1963.

From Germany, in 1965 we were posted back to Chelsea Barracks, London, from where I had last soldiered on my return from Russia eight years before, and found that a lot had changed since those days.

In 1957 'the Season' - culminating in Queen Charlotte's Ball in Grosvenor House - had been going on for 200 years. The Guards' Regimental Headquarters supplied debutantes' parents with the names of young officers, and the parents exchanged lists of other eligible young men, eliminating those who were deemed MTF (Must Touch Flesh) or VSITPQ (Very Safe in Taxis - Probably Queer).

My brother officers and I would get two or three white tie invitations every night, to these dinner parties and dances – but by 1958 the exclusivity of the Season had eroded. In the immortal words of Princess Margaret: 'We had to put a stop to it. Every tart in London was getting in.' But even so, Queen Charlotte's Ball was still to continue to flourish for another twenty years.

Unlike their modern counterparts *(whoops)*, back in 1957 young ladies did not so willingly drop their skirts after dessert, so young men would visit a renowned Mrs Featherstonhaugh (Ma Feathers) for a night of sexual relaxation. Ronald Ferguson is reputed to have had his 'first (*un*successful) sexual encounter there, with a naval officer's wife'. With my own sexual baptism at Ma Feathers, I have reason to suspect that I, too, probably failed to impress 'Detta', my partner on that occasion. (Now *there's* a confession for you!)

Postings to London meant finding Guards for the palaces, street lining, and of course the Sovereign's Parade.

In June 1768 there had been issued 'Orders for the General and Staff Officers . . . to meet the Duke of Cambridge on the Parade at Horse Guards at 10 o'clock on the morning of the King's Birthday, fully dressed in Embroidered Cloths'.

In June 1966 it was my privilege to command the Escort for the Colour at the Sovereign's Parade, when the Colours of the Irish Guards were being trooped.

Ensign for the Colour was Christopher Eugster, and the Subaltern was Robin Keigwin.

One faltering command, one mis-timed royal salute, or one bent line of march can make or break a parade like this.

It requires combined effort and determination to produce the very best, and for no man to let down his pals.

After the parade we repaired to St James's Palace, where Charles 1 had slept the night before his execution.

I am pleased to say that Her Majesty sent us her congratulations for a fine parade, which were passed on to all the Guardsmen.

All threats of executions were lifted, and the champagne corks popped.

Many memorable events occurred during this London tour of ours, but two of the most memorable were these - the first of which took place one day further inland . . .

At Otterburn, in Northumberland, in 1388, James Douglas and an army of 6,000 Scots attacked the English Army of 8,000, led by Sir Henry 'Hotspur' Percy.

As dawn broke the English ranks began to waver and retreat, Sir Percy was captured and Douglas slain.

In 1966, with peace prevailing with the Scots, I led my anti-tank platoon with our 17-pounders up to the wild and boggy training area of Otterburn.

The guns were pulled by 14cwt Stewart tracked carriers. During a training exercise one of my Stewart carriers sank in the bogs, and despite all efforts could not be recovered. It is still there to this day, deep below the peat, sharing its grave along with Douglas's kilted swordsmen.

It was my privilege to command the Escort for the Colour at the Sovereign's Parade, June 1966: Front L-R: the Author; Ensign for the Colour Christopher Eugster; Subaltern Robin Keigwin.

CHRISTMAS DAY IN THE RADFAN

Christmas in the Radfan – 1966: the GOC MELF
Sir John Willoughby's photo of a camel-borne Father Xmas
(the Author) about to deliver presents to the outlying picquets

46

L-R: C-in-C Middle East Admiral Sir Michael Lefanu; Political Officer Julian Paxton - and Author, on patrol in Dhala,

47

Stanley Services Boat Club, Hong Kong

The second 'event' had to do with a chap called Jespah.

It is a true 'dog story'.

My brother, Seymour, had asked me to look after his five-year-old black Labrador, Jespah, for a few days while he was away once.

I was on London duty at the time.

One morning, I led the New Guard from Chelsea Barracks to Buckingham Palace, where we performed the Guard Mounting Ceremony with the Old Guard, and then I marched with the Queen's Guard to St James' Palace.

My orderly had taken Jespah on to the St James' Palace Officers' Mess for me in the one-ton 'blanket' truck.

The following morning, before I dismounted the Guard at Buckingham Palace, I had my orderly escort Jespah from St James' Palace back to Chelsea Barracks in the one-ton truck again. When they reached Chelsea Barracks Jespah panicked and bolted from the truck, somehow or other managing to turn up much later at St James' Palace Officers' Mess where Robin Dixon, the new Captain of the Guard, deciphered his name and that of his owner on his collar, telephoned me to report his safe appearance, and put him into 'close arrest' until I arrived to collect him, delirious with relief and affection. (That's both of us!)

Jespah had walked a mile from Chelsea Barracks, probably down Ebury Bridge Road, Buckingham Palace Road, Queen Victoria Memorial, The Mall, and Stable Yard Road to the Officers' Mess at St James' Palace, without ever having walked or smelled the route before. My own scent (pungent aromatic after-glow – call it what you will), which was doubtless similar to his owner's, my brother Seymour, had been mixed with those of 40 soldiers of the Buckingham Palace and St James' Palace Guards, and then become considerably dispelled after the hour-long handing-over ceremony with the Buckingham Palace New Guard - but I can still think of no other possible explanation than that to this extraordinary canine story.

ELEVEN

- Aden -

IN 1421, CHINA'S MING DYNASTY EMPEROR, Yongle, ordered two of his principal envoys, the grand eunuchs Li Xing and Zhou Man to convey an imperial edict . . . *with hats and robes to bestow upon the king of Aden.*

The two envoys boarded three treasure ships and set sail from Sumatra, to the port of Aden.

The event was recorded in the book *Ying-yai Sheng-lan* by Ma Huan, who accompanied the imperial envoy.

In the 16th and 17th centuries Aden was occupied first by the Portuguese, and then the Ottoman Empire and Sultanate of Lahej, until in 1839 it was ceded to Great Britain and fell under the control of the British East India Company.

In 1966 Ist Bn Irish Guards arrived in Falaise Camp, in Little Aden, to protect the oil refinery staff against attacks by the Communists' National Liberation Front (NLF) and Front for the Liberation of South Yemen (FLOSY).

NLF fought FLOSY, and both these factions fought the British.

Whilst the Argyll & Sutherland Highlanders' commanding officer, Lt Col 'Mad Mike' Mitchell and his pipers were marching into Crater, my company and I were seconded to the Paras, in Sheikh Othman, a hotbed of NLF and FLOSY grenade attacks and sniping.

We were then moved up to Dhala, on the border with Yemen, where I wrote: *The commanding officer of the FRA (Federal Republican Army) to which we are attached, was*

50

killed when his vehicle passed over a Mark 7 mine. On March 31ˢᵗ at 2210 hours two loud explosions heralded a volley of small arms fire and Blindicide high-explosive anti-tank (HEAT) rockets, directed towards our camp. Our own mortars, machine-guns and troop of QDG (Queen's Dragoon Guards) roared into action and pounded the enemy positions. Later, I wrote: *In the last ten days at Dhala our camp has been attacked five times . . . Temple Hill picquet received five direct hits . . . a furious attack . . . Oliphant – the radar tracking device used by the Gunner troop attached to us, located enemy up the Turkish road.*

Commanding my company in Dhala I had two interesting visitors, whom we accommodated: these were Donald McCullin, who had come to photograph the Emir of Dhala in his palace below our camp, and Admiral Sir Michael Le Fanu, whom I led up the Jebel Jihaf with his SAS bodyguard.

Field Marshal Earl Alexander of Tunis, our revered Colonel, arrived in Aden to present us with our shamrock on St Patrick's Day.

On Christmas Day Major General Sir John Willoughby, the GOC-MELF (General Officer Commanding Middle East Land Forces) took a photograph (which was to become the regimental Christmas card) of *Major Gilbart-Denham, clad as Father Christmas, mounted on a camel, distributing gifts . . .*

In October the Battalion embarked on HMS Fearless, an assault landing ship, to carry out a dawn raid on Hauf, in the Yemen, where a rebel gang had been plaguing the local sultanate.

At 3 a.m. my company climbed into landing craft, and navigated for a mile and a half by the Special Boat Service, landed on Hauf beach – having been warned that our landing would be opposed.

Many of us landed in 5ft of water.

Fortunately no bullets came screaming at us when we scrambled drenched from the shore to run to our cordoning positions round the village.

Villagers were screened in a barbed wire enclosure, and we arrested 29 wanted men who we bound and helicoptered to the Sultan's gaol. With the Hauf tide falling, we were then flown back to Fearless.

It was from Aden that Christopher Wolverson, Peter Verney and I made a memorable visit up to Ethiopia.

For some part of our exploration we were accompanied by an acquaintance of Peter Verney, a Peter Fleming, who told us that his brother Ian would have been inspired to conjure up a 'Bond' thriller around the extraordinary treasures we saw in the Coptic churches there, and the primitive tribesmen in the Danakil Basin.

On our return to Aden I wrote a spoof article in our regimental *Harp* magazine, which was distributed locally and to the families at home.

Based on our adventures in Ethiopia, I wrote: *That day we slept until the sun went down, and then found we were guests of honour for a sumptuous feast at which the whole tribe was gathered.*

On my left was seated the fattest woman I had ever set eyes on.

According to local custom, a goat was led in, and whilst the animal was still alive meat was sliced off it, and eaten raw by the assembled guests. I was nauseated by this cruelty, but compelled to follow custom.

At the end of the feast Abbe asked me if I was satisfied with my wife.

I expressed astonishment, and was informed that by accepting coffee three times from a virgin, I had accepted betrothal. At that moment I felt a nudge behind me, and Major Verney pressed six small white pills into the palm of my hand. 'Sleeping tablets,' he whispered. 'Load her coffee!'

From Addis we motored to Mulu, the farm of Brigadier Stanford. During lunch, amidst a noise like thunder, Emperor Haile Selaisse arrived, escorted by a thousand horsemen, his imperial bodyguard. Imagine my surprise when, after a roll of native drums a thousand voices burst into the chorus of Iolanthe . . .

In Aden, Garry Daintry with his Sioux helicopter flew me miles around the country.

David Moore, our doctor, accompanied my platoons and me on countless 'Hearts and Minds' patrols, tending dysentery, burns, fractures and illnesses.

On 30th November 1967, after mass riots between NLF and FLSY – and 128 years there - the British finally pulled out of the place, and Aden became the capital of the new People's Republic of South Yemen.

TWELVE

– *Northern Ireland* –

IN SEPTEMBER 1968, in a Northern Ireland banned march that had been defied, the Catholic Campaign for Social Justice (CSJ) clashed with the Protestant Apprentice Boys of Derry.

Despite this ban on civil rights marches, there was another clash, on 1 January 1969, when at the Battle of the Bogside marchers were attacked by Protestants armed with iron bars, bottles and stones.

The Provisional Irish Republican Army emerged to defend the Nationalist community.

In 1968 I joined as Staff Captain 39 Brigade Headquarters in Lisburn, Northern Ireland.

My boss was Brigadier John Strawson, erudite and humane, with fearsome countenance.

Our headquarters was in Lisburn, where a one-time bard had written of the castle gardens there: *A bower of love and courtship, for the lads and lovely lasses . . .*

Thirty miles south of Lisburn lies the town of Newry, where between 1841 and 1852, my great grandfather, evangelist Joseph Denham Smith, preached and composed his 36 gospel hymns, tracts, pamphlets and small books. He worked in missions in Ireland, focussing on evangelism, before retiring as a pastor in Dublin.

When I first arrived all was peaceful, and I enjoyed driving to Donegal for deep sea fishing, trips to Dublin, and visiting friends around Eira.

However, all of that was to change, in August 1969, when British troops started patrolling the streets of Northern Ireland.

My younger brother, Seymour, arrived with a squadron of Life Guards, commanded by 'Bubbles' Fuller, and it was our happy task to find accommodation for them.

I wore two hats in my job: as the Headquarters Staff Captain, and Regimental Representative of the Irish Guards.

I enjoyed a close liaison with the 'Mini-Micks', an Irish Guards cadet unit in Lisburn, commanded by a Walter Mitty-ish character called Colin Wallace. Colin, in his official appointment of Public Relations Officer, Headquarters Northern Ireland, also worked for British Military Intelligence. He became involved investigating a homosexual scandal around the Kincora Boys Home, which was frequented by well known politicians - including Edward Heath.

Subsequently, tried in camera for 'shadowy misdemeanours', Colin received a three month prison sentence.

Details of the affair are clouded in mystery, but it was an embarrassment, it generally being felt that Colin must have been somewhat 'hung out to dry'.

I attended funerals of ex-Irish Guardsmen, one of whom was Colonel Conolly McCausland, a scion of one of the oldest Irish Protestant families, who had converted to Catholicism. His son, Marcus, who had joined the Ulster Protestant Defence Regiment, was later to be abducted by the IRA, put in a sack and bludgeoned to death. *Forty-two years later I was to receive a scroll recognizing my 20 years as a Putney School Governor. It was presented to me by the Mayor of Wandsworth, Councillor Piers Conolly McCausland - murdered Marcus's younger brother.*

A few years previously I had embarked on a great voyage of Ireland, staying with some of my fellow officers' parents: the McCauslands at 'Drenagh' in Co Derry, the Guinnesses at 'Lodge Park', Co Kildare; the Nugents, at 'Ballinlough House,' Co Westmeath; the Glentorans at 'Drumadarragh House', Co Antrim; the Blosse Lynches at 'Partry', Co Mayo - and General Verney, in Dublin.

Irish hospitality is second to none, but I remember especially two particular incidents.

On my visit to Powercourt with General Verney, his Lordship (Powercourt) told me that on one occasion when his great house was open to the public, he approached a family which he found picnicking under his drawing room windows, and politely asked them their name and where they came from.

A few days later . . . having travelled a little to reach their destination, their Lordships spread out a rug beneath that same family's small house, and started tucking into a picnic of their own!

On another occasion, staying at the huge house 'Drenagh', home of the McCauslands, I realised that Lady Margaret had little idea which of her guests were staying and which had gone, when she greeted one couple with: 'Oh, I thought you'd both left us two weeks ago!'

Many great houses always laid out an extra place for the unexpected guest. Curses by gypsies, and the starving during the famine, if they had been denied food, were also heeded and remembered.

John Strawson, my brigadier, was a hard but likeable taskmaster. 'I am not interested in your problems', he would say, 'only in how you overcome them.'

Aboard a Landing Craft Tank (LCT) heading for the Outer Hebrides, where 39 Infantry Brigade were to control an exercise, John became stuck in the lavatory when the door jammed. When it was opened, an hour later, he emerged quite unbothered. 'Officers should never be without a good book,' he said, - and he wasn't!

I saw a lot of an ex-Mick called Bill Hall (and his wife, Jennifer) - who was later to become a Lord Lieutenant. They had adopted a baby, and one day we all went for a boat ride on Strangford Loch. A violent storm blew up, and I was certain the boat was going to capsize. Miraculously, it didn't. But tragedy did occur later, on a ski trip to St Anton, with John Morrogh Bernard, a fellow Mick serving with me at 39 Brigade Headquarters. Skiing together in a 'white out' John fell down an abyss, disappeared and suffocated. It was with an exceedingly heavy heart that I bought his widow, Julia, back home.

And so, as Staff Captain, during the months of reviewing courts martial proceedings and officers' confidential reports, Northern Ireland continued to sizzle and erupt, and as in all civil wars, opposing factions adopted horrific tactics and perpetrations before, after many years of trouble, a peace accord was finally reached.

THIRTEEN

- The Far East -

AFTER THE FIRST OPIUM WAR and the Treaty of Nanking, in 1842, Hong Kong, the Fragrant Harbour, became a British Colony. !n 1898 Kowloon and the New Territories were ceded to Great Britain – on a 99-year lease.

In 1936 Stanley Barracks was built on the former site of a convalescent home. Later, the Royal Engineers built concrete emplacements there for three 9.2in guns.

In 1941 the Japanese invaded Hong Kong, and after bitter fighting, often without water, on Christmas Day the colony surrendered. Japanese soldiers entered nearby St Stephen's College, shot dead the two British doctors, and bayoneted all the wounded soldiers. They set up a beheading block in King's Park, Kowloon, and practised their bayoneting on the civilian population.

When I was there in 1970, I found that the command of Headquarters Company, for that was my appointment at the time, also entailed being the honorary secretary of Stanley Services Boat Club, which had naval, army and civilian members.

We had 14ft *Enterprise* and *Bosun* dinghies.

During the next two years, under the splendid stewardship of Charles Aikenhead and Sgt Moriarty, we managed to teach nearly every soldier in the battalion how to sail. We also persuaded 48 Ghurkha Squadron Royal Engineers to build us a new boat house.

Robert Corbett sold me his car, a black Sunbeam convertible, which served me well.

At that time members of Her Majesty's forces were not allowed to cross the border into China.

We provided picquets on the border, and at a place called Wo Lu, and would watch the trainloads of pigs arriving from China for the Hong Kong market, accompanied by the amplified songs and polemics of communist China. The Chinese had laid barbed wire and minefields along the whole stretch of the Hong Kong border, to deter their own people from entering the prosperous colony.

An incident that caused diplomatic eruptions was caused by one of my ration trucks and a Land Rover inadvertently taking a wrong road on the Shataukok border, and being bounced by local Hakka women over to China. The PLA (Peoples' Liberation Army) arrested the eight soldiers, but after giving them a good meal and accepting an apology from Sgt Skates, the senior soldier, released them all with their vehicles and weapons. In London, a Foreign Office spokesman announced: *'We are glad'* !

Typhoons were a regular occurrence in Hong Kong.

Whenever there was a typhoon warning we boarded up the windows and stayed indoors. Typhoon 'Rose' left the Macau ferry thirty feet up on the rocks, and started a mudslide on the island that turned houses and shacks upside down. Our Guardsmen assisted in the rescue, and Johnny Gorman later received the George Medal for heroically pulling trapped individuals to safety through treacherous tunnels of the collapsed houses.

On another occasion I took a party of Irish Guardsmen and Gunners up to South Korea and Japan, in HMS Intrepid. At Pusan, South Korea's southernmost port, we took on board a battle group of ROK (Republic of Korea) soldiers. The battle group was deployed on a beach landing exercise, but not before a significant amount of cutlery had disappeared from the lower mess room. The ship's commander mentioned this to the ROK adjutant, and soon afterwards the missing cutlery mysteriously reappeared. We later discovered that the ROK colonel told his men that any soldier found in possession of mess cutlery would be shot!

After a few days at Kobe, in Japan, I decided to travel up to Takayama, in the mountains. I stayed in a small guest house where that evening in the sitting room an elderly man was watching a samurai film on television. He ordered some sake for us both, clinked glasses, and ordered another bottle. And another. The following morning I awoke to find blood-stained tears in the paper walls, and my clothes, passport and wallet neatly stacked in the corner of the bedroom. Clearly I had passed out, and then fought like a cat on being undressed and put to bed by someone!

At breakfast I was informed that a delegation was on its way to see me.

Certain arrest, I thought.

The delegation duly +arrived.

It consisted of a gathering of university students who had heard of my prestigious consumption of sake the previous night, and the samurai-like tussle that had taken place with the proprietor, and after practising their English for a while, duly presented me with a Japanese sword and scabbard that bore their names.

In October, 1970, I escorted 52 musicians of the Irish Guards' Regimental Band, together with the Pipes and Drums, to Japan for a tour of Tokyo, Utsonomiya and Sasebo, Nagasaki, Unzen and Kumamoto, Fukuoka, Kitakyushu and Osaka, Kyoto, Toyama and Hiroshima, Himeji, Kobe and Nagoya, where we were to perform 32 concerts, travelling for four weeks by air, boat, train and bus.

The Author in attendance behind the Empress of Japan and her two daughters, Imperial palace, Tokyo – October 1970

The best sport was free diving to spear a giant grouper in its
hole. Charles Aikenhead having done just such, in Belize

The band played outside the large Nihonbashi Takashimaya store and, mobbed by children, marched through the streets.

We performed at the Imperial Palace, the first foreigners ever to do so. I sat in Tunic Order behind the Empress and her two daughters, the Crown Princess and Princess Chichibu. They were delighted with the performance, and especially with the piping and sword dancing.

We paraded at the Fuji TV studios, with children jumping up and down while the band played their favourite song *Ping Pong Pang.*

Accompanying our troupe was a delightful female announcer, 'Shina', who in typical oriental fashion could not pronounce her 'V's properly, so that over the microphone her *The Peanut Vendor* became *The Peanut Bender,* and with the persistent help of some of our bandsmen, eventually successfully seguing itself into *The Penis Mender!*

I have a fond recollection of Unzen, a hot spring resort we visited, where twenty kimono clad ladies poured tea and helped us undress into our 'yucata' light robes for the occasion.

The bubble burst on the day of our intended departure, when our impresario, Mr Kakuichi - a confidant of the Queen Mother – it was discovered had overreached himself, and we were confronted by his creditors, all lined up at the New Otani Hotel for payment.

Robin Duke and the British Embassy staff worked like Trojans to pacify and reassure them (they held the bus that contained the band's musical instruments), and finally managed to get us on the plane back to Hong Kong.

FOURTEEN

- Central America -

From the early seventeenth century the area in the Bay of Honduras known as Belize had had a troubled history. Privateers carried out raids against Spanish vessels transporting gold and silver, but by the end of the century this piracy had been suppressed, and the British settled in the coral reefs and sandbars-protected littoral and hinterland.

The small British settlement became a target for attacks from neighbouring Spanish settlements, which were repulsed by irregular militia and African slaves from Jamaica, and British warships.

The final skirmish against the Spanish occurred in 1798, in a sea battle off St George's Cay in which the local forces, supported by HM Merlin, forced a Spanish retreat.

But then came repeated clashes with neighbouring Guatemala, who refused to accept the status of Colony bestowed by Britain in 1862.

In 1964 Britain granted the colony internal self-government, retaining responsibility for defence and external relations, and providing a flight of fighter aircraft, ground attack aircraft and a battalion of infantry. This force stalled any warlike intentions from Guatemala, and at the same time provided an idyllic jungle training area for British troops.

It was to this Shangri-la that I arrived with the Irish Guards, in 1973.

Our flight took us via Keflavic in Iceland, and Gander, in Newfoundland, before we touched down in Belize, the tropical paradise of which Aldous Huxley once wrote: *If the world had any ends, then British Honduras would certainly be one of them.*

Our task there was to defend the country against its marauding neighbours, but it soon became apparent that Guatemalans seemed disinterested in any provocation, and under the command of Giles Allan, we settled in for a relaxed and adventurous tour.

I was still commanding Headquarters Company, which included the transport, catering, and signals elements for the Rifle and Support Companies in their different locations in this land of pine forests, mahogany trees, orchids, wild cotton and jungle, giving way on the coast to mangrove swamp.

The country's exotic hinterland was inhabited by deer, snakes and tapirs, jaguars, ocelots and 500 different varieties of birds, and while out training it was also possible for us to come across Mayan ruins or giant anthills.

The shallow waters around the cays within the Belize barrier offer some of the best diving in the world. Beyond the reef, some seven miles off shore, the depth of the sea plunges a whole mile. The reef protects the shallow waters where tarpon, grouper and bonefish, parrotfish, snapper and crayfish abound.

The cays could be and often were devastated during the hurricane season, but sometimes the aftermath of these events was an exciting reminder of the old days, when once again gold pieces of eight were brought to the surface!

Charles Aikenhead and Michael Warrender were the Masters of Diving, and taught me about air cylinders, demand valves, Boyle's Law, buddy lines and nitrogen narcosis, and eventually they passed me as being proficient as a British Sub Aqua Diver.

Every afternoon we boated out to St George's Cay or Gallows Point, spinning for barracuda, and diving.

Nurse shark, basking shark and sting ray patrolled the sandy bottom, and occasionally hammerhead and reef shark appeared, which is when we beat our hasty retreats.

We used bottles and spear guns, but the best sport was free diving, to spear a giant grouper napping outside its hole. Grouper and crayfish were then delivered to our cooks for a delicious evening meal.

Charles Aikenhead, Bru Bellew and I had a 16ft sail dinghy that we used to manoeuvre down the Belize River and mangrove swamp. Huge 4-metre-long manatee, or sea cows, bred in the river, and on one occasion the boat was nearly overturned when Henry Blosse Lynch couldn't resist poking his oar onto one of these dark shapes in the water that retaliated!

The Recce Platoon came under my command, and one day Brian O'Farrell invited me to join them down the Sibun River and gorge. Sometimes, wading through the catfish-infested river, at other times swimming with kit floating in 'air bag' ponchos, at other times scaling the ravines and battling through jungle, it was hard work, but a terrific exercise.

We were all airlifted home by 'chopper' after this exciting jungle and river 'bash'.

The people of Belize had as much variety about them as the terrain: Africans, Mayans and Caribs, Indians, Europeans and Chinese, Arabs and Mennonites.

Belmopan was the new purpose-built capital in the centre of Belize, and two interesting buildings in Belize were the 'Big C', a well-frequented brothel reputedly owned by a Government minister, and the Cathedral - reputedly built from the ballast in ships that brought the slaves. For adventures outside Belize there was a holiday resort at Merida in Mexico, and for those wishing to explore the Yucatan, trips to La Ceba in Spanish Honduras, or the Mayan ruined temples of Tikal, in Guatamala. If, as is unlikely, after descending into purgatory I arrive in heaven . . . then it's for certain sure that for my money I shall know where I'm at.

Belize!

FIFTEEN

' The Greek Islands -

IN 1973 MY YOUNGER BROTHER Seymour, Colin Crawford and Patrick Grayson all hired a caique in which to sail from Corfu to Paxos, a small island in the Ionian Sea.

Their cook was 'Flossie' - later to marry David Webb Carter.

When they reached Paxos, this colourful and piratical quartet met up there with an ex-Welsh Guards adjutant called George Richmond Brown, and an ex-sailor, Patrick May. These two were an enterprising couple who had set up a company they'd named Paxos General Investments (PGI).

After a good night out and a few drinks together, Seymour, Colin and Patrick collectively purchased from PGI a small plot of building land, just above the Paxos Beach Hotel.

Paxos lies within that rather 'sensitive' areas of Greece, which borders hostile Albania and Turkey. Only foreign companies with Greek directors on their boards were allowed to purchase land in these designated 'sensitive' areas.

When all parties had regrouped once more in England, rational discussion took place, the result being that for various reasons *I* bought up Colin's, Patrick's and Seymour's PGI shares from them.

The following year I returned to Paxos, where I arranged the purchase of a more suitable plot of land, above Balos Bay, and forwarded the money to have a very small villa built there.

And thus it befell that from those early days and those two percipient transactions, there began for me a life-changing saga which has endured over three decades.

The only way to get across from Corfu to Paxos was by means of an ancient and rusty ferry, the *Kemelia*, which took three-and-a-half hours, and rolled dreadfully.

My home, Villa Balos, was the only building between the Paxos Beach Hotel and Moganisi – and there was no road.

PGI, and Greek Island Villas (under Elliot Watrous), were the sole travel and land agents in Paxos.

There was one food shop there, run by a Zorba-like gentleman called Babis, and a hardware shop, where money could be exchanged.

There were few roads or cars, scooters being the main means of transport, one of which was on one memorable occasion responsible for me breaking my collar-bone.

Mother and my elder brother, Desmond, were to become frequent visitors, walking everywhere, enjoying the primitive conditions.

Life in Paxos and at Villa Balos was never easy.

The island was often battered by storms, which reduced the chairs in Gaios Square to tangled iron and matchwood.

Rats, euphemistically known as tree possums, created their nests and homes in the Balos rafters.

The sun warped its olive wood shutters.

Storms lifted the roof tiles, and because they contained no lining the tiles leaked anyway.

Because the pipes had been laid horizontally, the bathroom drains blocked.

Today the electricity comes from the mainland on cables across the ocean bed, but in my early days there it was repeatedly being cut off.

Rain water, which fed the sterna from roof gutters, often ran out, which meant importing water bowsers from the mainland.

Paxos – perennial guests included – Debbie Emerson

Carolyn Moore and Sue Bucknell

Earth for the garden terraces had to be brought in from Corfu.

One was unable to obtain kitchen utensils in Paxos, but as fast as we brought them out with us from England, Lydia the maid would pinch them.

The place was invaded by ants and mice.

And when we wanted to go swimming, it was often to find vicious little jellyfish swarming in Balos Bay.

In addition to all this hardship, I had my agents to contend with - Patrick and Katie May.

Patrick was a dishonest rogue with the accounts, with his distortion, duplication and invention of figures.

He and his wife, Katie, swore, shouted, and cursed each other, and even employed lawyers to deliberate over the division of their spoils.

Patrick eventually moved to Corfu, leaving Italian wife Katie behind in Paxos.

They corresponded only by telex.

Patrick then died of cancer, after which Katie's behaviour turned from eccentric to utterly demented.

One year I arrived there only to find that she had sold off the water in my villa's sterna, to the Head of the Electricity Board.

Another year when I got there, it was to see all my mattresses piled on the incinerator and that my chairs had been chopped up.

Enough.

I changed my agents to the Grammatikos family, of Paxos Magic Holidays.

Soon afterwards Katie May, too, was to die of cancer.

Amongst the contents of their house in Moganisi, 'Commander' Patrick May's RN discharge papers were discovered . . .

. . . upon which was recorded the year that 'Able Seaman' Patrick May had left the Royal Navy - to proffer tourism with dubious honesty on a Greek island.

My Paxos neighbours and friends included the ebullient Newton Webb Bowen, with his yacht *Dorothea;* Peter and Peggy Eriks, in their delightful Villa Aquamarine; Susannah York, the actress and film star; John Gough, founder of the Paxos Music Festival; perennial guests included Debbie Emerson and Carolyn Moore - and Richard and Audrey Coward, joint authors of the first ever walking guide to Paxos.

My principal challenge on Paxos is the on-going improvement of the villa.

Nearly every year some piece of remedial structure takes place, and between 1974 and 2010 practically the whole villa and garden were rebuilt and refurbished – usually by Albanian 'work horses', recruited like Roman gladiators from down in Gaios Square.

Whether swimming or walking, taking local bus rides in to Loggos and Lakka, or shopping in Gaios, supping in the tavernas or boating to Anti Paxos, life on the island is unique.

One never tires of walking on the island, with its honey scented broom, purple heathers, wild orchids and olive groves. It has 80 churches, azure green seas and grottoes which burrow into its limestone cliffs.

Yachts large and small, flotillas and ferries berth in the harbours of Gaios, Loggas and Lakka, providing lucrative business for all the bars and tavernas.

The Paxos International Music Festival, which is held each year in early September in Loggos, attracts talented musicians from Greece and beyond.

Ministers from Athens have come to confer in the Paxos Beach Hotel.

Mrs Agnelli, wife of the Fiat heir, has built her grand mansion in Moganisi.

A pair of Paxos-born millionaire brothers have built their marble palace in Gaios.

Paxos has a very special magic about it.

For thirty-five years, along with the Greeks who live on the island and the island's many visitors, I have been privileged to share much of that magic.

The Paxos Notary has registered ownership of Villa Balos to my nieces, Sophie and Georgie, enabling them to assume control when the time to do so befalls them.

SIXTEEN

- Ever the entrepreneur -

WHEN EVENTUALLY MY TIME CAME to leave the Army, in 1974, I teamed up with Duncan Vaughan Arbuckle, an ex-Queen's Royal Irish Hussar, and Colin Crawford, ex-Royal Horse Guards, to start a new enterprise: V. Arbuckle Ltd.

Duncan had years of experience in big business, and we were soon to start importing wines from France and Spain, sardines and mineral water from Portugal, and other delicacies from around the world.

We rented a warehouse, underneath the BR arches at Covent Garden, where we housed £1M's worth of our wine.

We bought the Midnight Shop in the Brompton Road, and the John Gare pub in Crawford Street.

All this adventurous, exciting, hair-raising stuff was done with money borrowed from the banks.

Duncan, Colin and I started by distributing the wine in our cars to our customers, who were wine bars, pubs and hotels, while Duncan's wife, Vicky, did all the invoicing and accounts.

Soon we bought a number of vans and employed stalwart Kiwis to do our driving and delivering for us.

Sir Patrick Cormack MP's brother, Willie, became our head salesman

I then peeled off to run the Midnight Shop by myself, strategically located near Harrods, and the first delicatessen in London to remain open till midnight.

We inherited a number of managers and staff there, who worked in shifts from 9.00 a.m till midnight.

I did the supervision, PAYE, accounts, and stock control, and after checking the till-slips each morning, deposited the takings in the bank.

In spite of our security cameras, we still experienced problems: shop-lifting customers; staff either pinching or failing to record items sold; air conditioning that was unable to cope with the fridges, and evening smash and grab robberies on our tills.

On a number of occasions I had to apprehend thieving customers and summon the police. Often the culprit was a titled lady, who seemed to think it was her right to conceal her purchases.

One morning I found the safe completely empty of the night's takings, but although it was only the three managers who knew the safe's combination, the police were still unable to nail the culprit.

In November 1979 V. Arbuckle Ltd fell insolvent, was heavily in debt, and was sold to Charles Wells for the sum of £1.

Soon afterwards Duncan, who was always the architect of grandiose schemes, and usually something of a disaster at implementing them, devised a plan for a Museum of Wine. This idea was sold to Sandy Anderson, a Scottish entrepreneur who poured millions into converting BR arches in Southwark into 'Vinopolis - City of Wine' - establishing what is now a major attraction in London, with a turnover of over £10,000,000 a year. Duncan, who was initially a Board member, was soon sacked.

SEVENTEEN

- Banged up -

THERE ARE NOT MANY EX-GUARDS OFFICERS who can claim to have appeared in the dock at Reading Assizes.

I was one who did.

Unlike the unfortunate Oscar Wilde though, I walked away free.

Nor did I even compose a ballad afterwards.

This is what happened . . .

Sometime in 1979 I read in *The Times'* 'Personal' column about someone who was seeking ambitious aspirants prepared to invest £2,000 in a flourishing holiday travel company, and become working partners.

A group of us, including some other ex-officers, replied to the advertisement.

Subsequently we were all invited to attend a meeting in a five star hotel.

There was already a brand new Rolls-Royce parked outside the front entrance when we arrived.

That's where we were to meet the founder of the company, the owner of the Rolls-Royce - John Knox.

We were shown an impressive film about Holiday Companionship, (the name of the company), an outline of its operations, and its success in recruiting, finance and turnover.

The idea was that the company would provide the expertise, literature, flights and accommodation, and the partners – us - at our own expense, all the necessary local venues and advertising to attract members of the general public to our briefing meetings.

The name of the game was travel and companionship for single people.

The company had identified a niche in the market.

The Rolls-Royce provided the evidence of that success.

It was a winner!

So we left the meeting, and for the ensuing few months advertised locally, arranging group meetings in pubs, hotels and in our own houses.

There was just one problem.

Few people responded.

We representatives contacted each other, and came to the conclusion that we were all the victims of a con.

A fellow colleague, a former Inland Revenue Officer, asked me whether I would be prepared to give a statement to this effect, to the SIB, and I agreed that I would.

This is why one year later I was to find myself the principal Witness for the Prosecution against John Knox, and his co-conspirators, at Reading Assizes.

Despite claiming in his defence he suffered from claustrophobia, and that jail would kill him, Knox went down for a hefty sentence.

None of us ever got any of our money back, of course, much of which, it transpired, had gone to help support John Knox's mother in her declining years - maybe with some travel and companionship thrown in for the old girl, for good measure!

EIGHTEEN

- Oily old Brian -

IN 1980 OIL WAS STILL UNDISPUTEDLY REFERRED to as Black Gold, so I decided that it was now about time in my life for me to go and tap some of it for myself, off Aberdeen, and thereby gain a belated foothold as an 'oil man'.

There follows some some notes of my time on the rigs there:-

With an oil worker called Harry, I left the Aberdeen Company Boarding House and walked across to the pub. A few introductions and drinks later and we were sitting in the Volkswagen bus, moving to the heliport.

'Although the Norskies (Norwegians) own it, it's the Texans who run the rig,' explained Harry, 'and them Yanks have learnt a thing or two from us, too, since they started . . . '

I looked up, waiting to hear some jewel of technological information about dehydrogenation or furfural extraction, but what I got was . . .

'They used to allow us only five minutes' tea break, but they bloody soon learnt that a British tea break lasts fifteen minutes at least!'

The inside of a Sikorkski helcopter is not dissimilar to a London bus, and accommodates about the same number of people.

Soon this monstrous leviathan was slicing its way through the skies.

One-and-a-half-hours and two-hundred miles later it began hovering over a cluster of orange marker buoys.

Our rig.

WAAGI 1.

The wheels of the chopper touched down.

Icy wind rushed in through the door.

My life as an oil rig roustabout was about to begin.

The Mud Room on a rig is not a room, and it does not contain mud.

It is a vast shed, which contains sacks of resinex that blackens you, dehydrated lime that blinds you, and caustic soda that burns you.

These sacks arrive in containers from the supply ship.

It is then the job of the roustabouts to heft the sacks out of the containers onto pallets.

Young Stevie drove his fork lift truck, catching and tearing the plastic covers of the chemical sacks.

Then we roustabouts shovelled up the spilled blinding, burning blistering and blackening crystals, and fed them to the fishes.

After lunch we gathered on deck for our fresh orders.

'Major,' my crane operator boss said to me, amicably delighting in our role reversal. 'You go and get the steam machine going, and then clean the outside of the dungeons'.

I knew what and where the Dungeon was, that deep recess in the rig leg where the bolts, chains, ropes and heavy paraphernalia are stored.

The steam machine was like an octopus, with its tentacles connected to power sockets, air sockets, and tin barrels where the cleaning brew was concocted.

At an early stage in the proceedings my steam hose suddenly started to have a violent altercation with the barrel, and was writhing and thrashing about like an infuriated python.

It was at this moment that George, the welder, chose to stick his head into the dungeon door, and shout: 'FIRE!'

Not wishing to lose out on my rig medal for gallantry, I redirected my octopus tentacle promptly towards the pinpricks of flame he was referring to, which were absolutely no match for my hissing steam machine . . .

. . . and so George's fire was duly doused.

A roustabout's life was rather fun, when there were things to do, like 'running the casing', 'tripping in' and 'tripping out' (mucking about with the pipes that go down the hole), and offloading stores from the supply ship.

But more often than not there was nothing positive that needed doing.

One morning, when the North Sea was offering a swirling cocktail of snow, sleet, hail and rain, the Pusher called us roustabouts out into the Force-7 gale to swab the helideck.

Precariously we ascended the helideck's ladder with our mops and buckets, clinging on to the railings for dear life, and sloshed about squeegee-ing the place until the driving sleet entirely obliterated our rather pointless efforts.

There are two activities continuously in operation on an oil rig.

Swabbing and painting.

The paint foreman kept an armada of paint in his stores; never had it been known in the history of oil exploration for a foreman ever to run out of paint.

Jock, our foreman, eyed his reluctant recruits suspiciously. 'Major', he said, handing me a paint tray and roller, 'you git rolin' on the starb'd catwalk, if you would, please'.

'Aye, Jock,' said I, stepping from the paint store out into the howling wind lashing around the catwalk in every direction.

I opened my jaws to tighten the strap securing my safety helmet.

Holding on to the ladder I dipped my roller into the battleship grey paint.

My roller rolled against the metal panels.

The wind caught the paint, which then flew away like flotillas of dandelion seeds.

Soon my arms, face and clothing were smothered in battle ship-grey pox.

Jimmy, the chef, happened to pass, and seeing this strange apparition perched on a swaying ladder, cried: 'Major – perhaps you should have given yourself an undercoat first!'

I tried hard to reply, but my eyes and mouth were covered in too much paint.

Seeing my predicament, Jimmy led me from my perch and steered me towards the leeward gash area, where he attempted to clean me up with turpentine and rags.

He then smeared my face with butter.

'This is the painter's best friend', he volunteered. 'A little butter will protect you from the clutches of Madame Tussauds!'

Food in the rig's galley was excellent.

We queued up with divers, engineers and drillers, radio operators and the Captain, to collect our shrimp cocktails, T-bone steaks, scampi Provençale, boeuf Stroganoff, and strawberry flan.

We then repaired to the rest room either to watch films, play darts or listen to safety lectures.

Having completed our required 14-day 12-hour stints, we were then 'choppered' off back to Aberdeen, where we were paid off and provided with a rail ticket to our port of choice.

The pay envelopes of the welders, tool pushers and drillers were far fatter than than those of us roustabouts.

And they had much less grey paint on their faces.

NINETEEN

− A greener shade of khaki − my life as a Middle East mercenary −

RETURNING FROM MY FINAL STINT on our North Sea platform, between Aberdeen and Stavanger, my thoughts had switched from digging for oil, to the possibility of doing some more soldiering *on* it – out in one of the Gulf States.

I applied for a job in the Sultan of Oman's Armed Forces (SAF).

I had commanded a company of Micks out in Aden, and had learned some useful Arabic phrases there, such as 'Halt - *Waqqaf!*'

'Surrender - *Istaslim!*'

And 'What is your tribe? - *Aysh Qabea Latak?*'

But after nine years out of uniform I suspected that I might be a little rusty on my tactical deployment and ambush drills.

I needn't have worried.

After some administrative correspondence I was not asked to reincarnate myself as a gung-ho warrior leader after all, but was offered the far more sedentary post of mess manager at the garrison officers' mess in Muaskar-al-Murtafa'a, known locally as MAM.

MAM was the Oman Army's equivalent of Aldershot, located near Oman's Seeb International Airport.

My contract was to serve there for two years, in the rank of Naqib (Captain).

I accepted.

At about this time an erstwhile colleague of mine, David Tomson, had invited me to become Director of an import/export company he was forming, dealing with Nigeria, which, too, was rich in oil!

David had inherited a lot of money from his family brewery, Tomson & Wotton, the oldest privately owned brewery in England, founded in Ramsgate, in 1634.

Over the next twenty years I was to attend discussions, lunches and dinners with Nigerian Chiefs from Abuya, Emirs from Kano and more Chiefs from Yoruba.

David was to pour his money into designing and selling police uniforms to Nigeria, fast patrol boats, 'Wizza' 150cc motorcycles, 'Moova' 200cc 4-stroke load carriers, and hundreds more products besides.

But sadly, with little success.

Even more sadly, it was at this time that my elder brother Desmond suddenly and tragically died of a heart attack, whilst out walking his dog, in Wandsworth. Desmond was a 50-year-old retiree from stock broking, within which profession he had operated in both London and Canada. I broke the distressing news to my mother, who was herself suffering courageously with cancer, in her house in Chobham, from which four years later she, too, was to die.

Concurrently, my younger brother Seymour was beginning to make cooing noises, and I realised that a result of his nesting would soon be the sale of our jointly owned house in Vardens Road, Wandsworth.

Amongst my lodgers in Vardens Road were my cousin, Francis Kinsman, and Judy Smith - who were to become my closest friends . . . and then marry each other!

In anticipation of Seymour's forthcoming nuptials therefore, I bought for myself a tenanted property in Putney, renovated its ground floor, and moved in temporarily with a Mrs Phelps, with her outside privy, and a tin bath on the staircase. However, more of this later . . .

Gulf Air flew me out to Oman, where I was to remain for the next two years: 18-months in MAM as the garrison officers' mess manager, and six months as second-in-command to the Oman Army's Training Company, at a remote outpost called Saiq, up in the Jebel Akhdar mountains.

These were to be two of the best years of my life, marred only by a severe personality clash with and the unpleasant machinations of an over-promoted MAM Garrison Commander, one ex-Green Howard, ex-Oman Gendarmerie Lt-Col Nick Mander, who was my boss there. Not for nothing was his nickname 'Biffo'.

A quarter century later I chanced to find myself sitting next to 'Biffo' in church, at a colleague's funeral. He didn't recognize me, and apologized that he had no recollection whatsoever of any incident I related to him, making me assume that he was probably suffering some early onset dementia.

At the Headquarters in MAM one of my less onerous duties was playing tennis with General Sir Timothy May Creasey, Deputy Commander-in-Chief and Chief of the Defence Staff, in his delightful official residence with tennis court, swimming pool, and tea served by stalwart Omani orderlies.

The General, nicknamed 'The Bull', told me that in 1955 he very nearly changed his career to that of big game hunter, when he was Brigade Major to 39 Infantry Brigade in Kenya.

General Tim played a cunning spin at tennis, but was sadly to die of cancer shortly after leaving Oman.

The officers' beach club was run by Major Bill Foxton, an ex-Green Jacket, ex-French Foreign Legion character who deftly handled a left hook instead of a hand, on what was left of his mine-blown arm.

The beach club was a great retreat from the soaring Arabian heat. There one could swim, windsurf, sail, dive or simply quaff a cool, refreshing can of Heineken, for some reason known by the boys as a Green Monkey.

Most afternoons I spent there windsurfing, under the tutorage of my cousin, an ex-9th Lancer, Lt-Col Jeremy Rawlins - or else sub-aqua diving with the delightful ex-SAS Lt-Col Roger Woodiwisss.

Occasionally I would take over the beach club from Bill Foxton, when he went on leave.

We were all shattered when twenty-five years later this larger-than-life colourful character, Bill, tragically shot himself in the head with a revolver on a park bench in Southampton, after losing all his money to the American fraudster, Bernie Madoff, in the financial scandal that rocked the world.

I flew to Salalah, and looked down to Hauf, in the Yemen, where ten years previously I had commanded no 1 Company Irish Guards, in Special Boat Services' RIBS (Rigid Inflatable Boats) from HMS Fearless, to apprehend rebel tribesmen.

I attended some of the sumptuous feasts Sultan Qaboos held in some of his several palaces, when the best hotels prepared lobsters, fillet steak and venison, veal, duck, and sweets with mountains of cream, all laid out on long lines of tables on the expansive green lawns.

As soon as His Majesty departed these affairs, his Royal Guard would dash in with bin liners and stuff into them the remains of the food: turkey, hams, and ice cream, tarts, prawns and lamb chops, asparagus and cheese crackers to take home to their wives and children.

Once a year Sultan Qaboos would go out from his Muscat palace to dispense 'instant hands-on government' at tribal gatherings around the country, going 'walkabout' to anywhere from Musandam in the extreme north, to Murbat in the far south.

He and his entourage (majlis) travelled in a convoy of 4-wheel-drive vehicles, and a magnificent and enormous tent was pitched for him at each stop.

From the air this tent in the desert resembled some giant lily in a pond.

Sultan Qaboos was a remarkable man who, with Oman's oil revenue, transformed a poor, illiterate and backward country into an educated and prosperous nation.

The following three accounts of life in Oman are taken from letters I wrote home:-

The garrison officers' mess at Muaskar-al-Murtafa'a is an imposing fortress type building, bedecked with electric light bulbs, and standing stolidly in a sea of desert.

Hibiscus, jacaranda and bougainvillaea adorn the small gardens, tennis court and swimming pool around the area.

A gardener, weary from his Ramadan fast, lies asleep like a caterpillar, curled under a date palm.

Another, more vigorous, deftly waters the acacia.

The sweet smell of frangipane enriches the hot air.

Inside the great doors of the garrison mess, a large picture of HM the Sultan Qaboos greets the visitor.

Ancient rifles adorn the high white walls.

The dull purr of air conditioning converts the outside blistering heat to a beautiful cool temperature.

The rooms are huge, and the floors marbled or carpeted.

There is a TV room, video room, billiards room and table tennis room, a reading room, dining room, and a bar serving soft drinks.

Waiters dressed with long white 'dishdasha' and 'masar' glide silently from room to room, serving, sweeping, tidying and cleaning.

Mess members include mainly British, Omani and Pakistani officers, civilians from the Oman Ministry of Defence, Sri Lankan doctors and dentists, and Egyptian and Jordanian teachers and interpreters.

I have 105 Baluchi, Omani, Pakistani, Indian and Sri Lankan staff, which include 24 cooks, accountants and clerks. They are intensely loyal and hardworking. I also have a British warrant officer as my assistant, and a British ACC (Army Catering Corps) warrant officer.

Omani curry and English food are served together in the dining room.

The Christian cooks from Goa cook the pork.

Omanis prefer the mild curry, the Indians and Pakistanis the hot curries.

The Egyptians have three times the appetite of all the others.

It is the duty of the mess manager to resolve the national preferences and exercise the understanding of Allah.

Once a month I oversee a barbecue by the pool.

Immaculately attired mess staff serve succulent meats, fish and sweets from white-sheeted long trestle tables, while guests sit on individual tables around the pool.

It is my job to supervise the purchase and entitlement of alcoholic drinks to the Omani officers - the higher the rank, the greater the entitlement. The teetotal Sultan himself has decided the quota.

Accommodation lies outside the mess.

The officers' quarters (bayts) are comfortable and air-conditioned.

It is not my duty to inspect inside them.

Some members of Bedouin extraction cook their meals in their 'bayts', and keep their wives and children there as well. And sometimes perhaps even their camels?

The world soccer championships are eagerly followed, and watched on Gulf TV.

This evening an enthusiastic gang of members collected in the TV room for the Brazil v Italy match, only to find that the game was not being relayed to Arabia or the Gulf, because the umpire was Jewish.

On alternate nights there is a film show up on the flat mess roof under the stars, when the temperature will have dropped into the 90s or mid-80s, and there is a whisper of a breeze. The camp is alive with a hundred thousand lights and the heavens with a million stars.

The Jebel Akhdar in Northern Oman rises to 3,000 metres and contains some of the most spectacular scenery in all of Arabia.

Between 1957-59 this region was the scene of intense fighting between SAS-supported Omani forces, and Saudi Arabian-backed rebels.

The tribesmen are fierce and independent, the country rugged and inhospitable.

When Major John Jackson, an ex-Greenjacket (whom I knew had lost his lower leg on a mine in the Dhofar war of 1970-75) invited me to stay with him for a couple of days at the Sultan's Armed Forces Training Centre (SAFTR) he commanded up there at Saiq, in the heart of the Jebel Akhdar, it was an invitation I could not refuse.

Getting there entailed two hours early-morning driving from Seeb, through Bidbid and Iski, through the Wadi Mudgin and past the Old Fort, until my Toyota and I arrived at a manned barrier and the gateway to the Jebel Akhdar.

The Jebel Akhdar is a restricted area, and a signed pass is needed by anyone wishing to enter there.

An Omani 'jundee' (soldier) asked me my name, made a quick radio call, and bade me park my car and climb into his Land Rover with him.

For the next hour we climbed and snaked our way up through gorges and ravines, carving our way higher and higher into the solid grey mountains. One error of judgment and the driver and his vehicle (with me aboard, remember) would plummet thousands of feet down the jagged mountainside.

The air became cooler and dryer.

We arrived finally at an open air plateau with a sign displaying 'SAFTR Advanced Training Company SAIQ'.

A central compound of buildings comprising offices, MT and accommodation dominated the area, and to the flanks were pitched two hundred or so tents.

John Jackson was there to welcome me, and invited me to accompany him to the jundees' breakfast, where they were joyously about to celebrate the end of the Muslim Fast of Ramadan and the celebratory commencement of their Eid al Fitr jollifications.

The jundees, clutching their rifles, were gathered under a reed awning, and stood up as we approached. We shook hands with each of them, exchanging 'salaams', and sat down cross-legged in the rectangular gathering.

Strongly spiced goat meat with rice and raisins were presented in wide circular bowls.

Taking care not to present the souls of our feet, and leaving dormant the 'unclean' left hand, we kneaded together the rice and meat, and lustily set to eating.

The goat meat was tender and delicious, and the rice succulent, dry and tasty.

Then came the halwa, a favourite Arab sweet, flavoured with saffron.

Finally Arab coffee in small cups was served - three cups, and no more!

Abruptly the 'fuddal' (for this is what such a picnic is called) ended, the recruits stood up, clasped their rifles again, and wandered off to their respective tents.

Time came for me to meet the only other resident European in the Akhdar plateau, the Jebel Liaison Officer, an ex-Gurkha officer called Graham Vivian.

Graham's house was built of fine local stone, balanced on the escarpment overlooking the Akhdar 'Rift Valley', and must have enjoyed one of the finest views in all of Arabia.

We swam in his ice-cool pool, fed from a nearby spring, consumed a few ice-cool beers, and then headed off towards some of the villages, on this first day of Eid Al Fitr.

Bani Habib is a typical Akhdar village, built on the side of a mountain, with rectangular stone houses cemented with mud and straw.

Below are terraced fields fed with water from springs or wadis, transported via the ancient 'falange' irrigation system, which had been introduced hundreds of years ago by Oman's Persian invaders.

Stepping through the narrow dusty passages of Bani Habib we met men and boys always eager to shake hands and exchange the customary greeting 'Salaam Alaikum'.

The women, finely adorned with silver ear rings, silver necklaces and silver head pieces, and clothed with cottons of purple, green and magenta, scuttled away in the presence of any stranger – and the inconsiderate pointing of a camera might even initiate a diplomatic incident.

We were ushered into a richly carpeted guest room, and squatted down with some elders who wore traditional white gowns with silver-encrusted daggers, or khunjars, tucked into their belts.

First of all dates were produced, followed by bowls of water served by small grubby boys, for us to wash our hands. We were then proffered the obligatory three cups of coffee, goat meat, bread, three more cups of coffee, more grubby small boys with bowls of water, local oranges, peaches and grapes, and finally three more cups of coffee.

During the meal John was conversing fluently in Arabic the whole time.

The sky started to darken and rain to fall, gently at first, then heavily.

Soon great cascades of water were running into the wadis. This was the first rain to fall there in four months.

'Jump into the wagon,' John said. 'I need to see how much of the road has been washed away'.

We did not have to travel far to see the results of the rain. Torrents of water surged over stretches of the road with dislodged boulders, and in places the road had disappeared completely.

That evening the Vivians were invited to our barbecue in the mess.

As we were preparing the charcoal fire a Toyota Land Cruiser appeared in the mess yard.

Inside were four Australians from the Oman Ministry of Agriculture.

The two in the back seats were bloody and bruised, their vehicle having overturned in the flash flood.

They were lucky to be alive!

On another occasion, back in MAM:

'I shall be launching my balloon tomorrow morning', the Queen's Royal Irish Hussar Charles Weston Baker said to me. 'It will mean a very early start. Would you care to come along?'

I needed no second invitation.

Charles had just taken excited delivery of his gas-fired, single-seat balloon from England - probably the first ever to be launched over Oman.

At 4.30 next morning Charles thumped on my bedroom door.

In ten minutes I was dressed and ready to go.

We drove through the dark to the Armoured Regiment's camp outside Seeb, and there met up with our ground crew, Tim Coombe, Royal Tank Regiment, Jim - a captain from the US Army, and Commander John Lane, Royal Navy - his wife, Manda, and their three children.

Our three cars' headlights illuminated the assembly area.

As we extracted the balloon from its bag and started sorting out the guide ropes, Charles explained that ballooning has to be done early in the morning, before the outside ambient temperature builds to exceed the heat within the balloon.

With the gas cylinder secured beneath the seat, the balloon guide ropes harnessed to the seat frame and the static rope line fixed to the tubular seat, we shook the heavy balloon material to fill it with cold air.

My turn came.

I climbed aboard, donned my crash helmet, secured the seat belt and opened up the throttle.

With a further roar of gas and a flame like the 'burn off' of an oil rig, the balloon rose aloft, a few hundred feet above the Armoured Regiment camp.

It's straining to be free of its static line,' Charles shouted up from the ground while the ground crew hauled me back down to mother earth again by yanking the line in, 'so now you're going to see some free flying'.

Removing the static line Charles clambered into the seat.

With an explosion of gas he was off!

We watched him disappearing into the tinted sky, and climbed aboard our cars to give chase.

Through the scrub and along the wadis, over the sand dunes we followed the balloon's flight.

Eventually, with the sun beginning to light and warm the landscape we reached our quarry, just as the beautiful balloon began gently descending to rest.

Tim and Jim hung onto its frame.

Charles stepped out.

Next it was my turn, to fly solo for real this time.

Helmet; gloves for protection against the searing heat – my camera, and some courage.

Throttle fully down, a volcanic flame, and I was airborne.

The sun was starting to warm up.

I remembered that if the ambient temperature rose too much the balloon might be in difficulties.

I was also nearing the end of my gas supply.

Too much heat from the sun meant too much gas from my cylinder.

Too little gas, and she would candle.

Up, up she went.

The ground crew disappeared beneath me as tiny dots in the sand.

Seeb village below seemed like a toy town.

Life as an oil-rig roustabout can be fun, what with 'running the casing', 'tripping in' and 'tripping out …

"I think that probably we must be somewhere . . . *here!* *(Insh-allah)*." Omani army officers on a map reading exercise.

Throttle fully down, a volcanic flame and John Lane (RN)
was airborne

Troubadours Martin Crossley and the Author 'entertain' the diners in Belgrano
District on South American cricket tour - 1989

Soon aircraft would be taking off from nearby Seeb airport.

A balloon would not fare well in the slipstream of a Boeing 707.

Perfect, perfect peace as my balloon and I floated high above the desert dunes.

I reduced the gas heat, and the canopy luffed.

I began slowly losing height.

But the earth was still coming up towards me rather too quickly, so I gave the throttle a long pull to create more heat.

Twenty seconds later and a few yards from the ground, the balloon began rising again into the air.

The ground crew scrambled once more into their vehicles to continue the chase.

Goats and chickens in Seeb village panicked as the balloon towered above them.

Then the wind caught us, and we floated away faster than the cars could follow.

With little gas to spare I luffed the canopy again, and slowly brought her down once more.

Crunch!

Our trusty crew were there, hot and tired from the chase, but ready to secure the balloon.

As the sun started to rise and bathe the desert in its hot iridescent glow, we disassembled the balloon and packed up the pieces into the back of a Toyota van.

A champagne, yoghurt and poached eggs breakfast brought an end to a truly amazing morning.

TWENTY

- *Interim in London* -

BEFORE LEAVING ENGLAND FOR OMAN I had let out the ground floor of my tenanted house, 20 Gladwyn Road, to a Mrs St Clair-Johns, who at the time was manageress of the Oxfam shop in Putney.

When I returned from my two year Oman assignment in 1985, it was to have Mrs St Clair-Johns declining to move out of number 20, saying she had no money, and nowhere to go.

This resulted in my being obliged to employ my cousin, Hugo Page, as counsel, and taking Mrs St Clair-Johns to Wandsworth Court.

Because she had applied for legal aid, it was the state which provided counsel for her defence.

The case, which I won, lasted four days.

Mrs St Clair-Johns was instructed to leave 20 Gladwyn Road, and to pay me her arrears of rent.

Had I lost the case, I would have been called upon to pay my own and the state's legal costs, but even though I had won I was still unable to recover my £2,000 legal costs.

As Hugo reminded me, justice and the law are strange bedfellows.

The Central Office of Information (COI) is the Government's marketing and communications agency.

It is a non-ministerial department, an executive agency that recovers its costs from other departments.

I applied for a job with them, which was to escort Foreign Office overseas VIPs around London.

We had important visitors from all over the world; bankers, journalists and economists, politicians and industrialists whom we escorted to the Home Office, Foreign Office, Houses of Commons and Lords - restaurants, theatres and multiple government departments.

On one occasion I took a visitor to the *Daily Mirror* Fleet Street offices where I met the then renowned agony aunt and columnist (Dear Marje) the late Marjorie Proops, whom I thought delightful.

After each assignment we were required to write a report, with emphasis on the visitor's reactions in any meetings and discussions.

The worst of our visitors were the Nigerians, who seldom kept to any appointment.

The best? They were from the Far East, and were always punctual, well dressed, considerate and polite.

Any gifts we received (particularly from the Arabs) we had to declare and hand in, sometimes being allowed to purchase the item later at a discounted price!

However, there were problems with this means of employment, principally that our assignments were sketchy and poorly remunerated, so in spite of it being a fascinating job, after two years I quit.

To keep the wolf from the door, next I attended a number of house auctions.

Residences with protected tenants in them sold for much less than even half the normal market price.

At these auctions I found myself intimidatingly up against orthodox Hasidic Jews, with their Hebrew 'kippah' scull caps over their long hair locks.

Viewing the houses from the catalogues beforehand was also difficult, because the elderly residents tended to ignore door knocks and door bells, so our buying was done 'blind', the principal determining factor in each case being the property's location.

The need was then always justifiably anticipated for the property to have to undergo a complete renovation as soon as the resident had departed.

I purchased for myself four houses in this way, at auction. One was in Gladwyn Road, SW15 (before I left for Oman) and then, when I returned two years later, three in Pages Walk, SE1 - each of which cost me between £16,000 and £18,000.

I found an excellent surveyor in Peter Caselton, who was to become a long established friend.

Mrs Phelps, whom I'd left still living in the other part of 20 Gladwyn Road, died while I was in Oman, and the three residents in my Pages Walk properties I subsequently re-housed with Bermondsey Council.

I still live today in number 20 Gladwyn Road.

All the Pages Walk houses, previously owned by British Rail, had now been acquired and were in the process of being renovated, and the area was becoming quite transformed.

Most days I would go down to Bermondsey to oversee their building works, being visited there about once a week by Peter Caselton, who monitored developments.

In 1988 I was able to sell two of the houses at a considerable profit, and then my cousin, Jeremy Rawlins, with whom I had served in Oman, persuaded me to go out to join him selling timeshare at Los Gigantes, in Tenerife.

Los Gigantes is probably the nicest resort in all of Tenerife.

It enjoys a beautiful location, situated on high cliffs overlooking the sea, with excellent shops and restaurants, and a number of timeshare companies selling apartments there.

We salespeople were expected to find our own accommodation, and were paid by results.

The perception of timeshare was to change for the worse over the years, but at that time the acquisition of a timeshare apartment was a good buy: I even bought one for myself!

Compared with Jeremy I was a very poor salesman, but I found the interaction between buyer and seller fascinating, learning to read body language and to employ the devious techniques of selling.

It was whilst I was in Los Gigantes that I received a telephone call from an ex-Mick chum of mine, Martin Carleton-Smith, who was now a property developer in Rotherhithe and Bermondsey.

'Would you be prepared to sell your remaining house in Pages Walk to my partner?' he asked me – so seeing no reason not to, I did.

After twelve months of enjoying fantastic weather, great swimming, great food, enjoyable company and a wealth of selling experience, I decided it was time to quit the Canaries and head back home once more.

TWENTY-ONE

- South of the border -

IN 1989 BARNEY MILLER invited me to join his cricket team of 'Troubadours' as their scorer, touring Argentina and Brazil.

The tour lasted three weeks.

There were 15 players, including professionals such as Simon Hinks, and county players John Carr, Chris Farrel and Daniel Kelleher.

We put on four shows, inspired and led by Cambridge 'Footlights' guitarist and singer Barney, with his wife, my old Hovingham school chum, Diana.

Back home in London afterwards, I spoke at the Mountbatten Hotel on the occasion of the Old Georgian (Argentinian) Society dinner.

Here's how it went:-

'Ladies and Gentlemen:

'It now seems 'de rigeur' for the Troubadours' scorer to address the Old Georgian Society, and let you know what really went on behind the screens in Argentina and Brazil. Being no cricketer, and certainly no scorer, climbing aboard the 747 at Amsterdam for Buenos Aires, armed with pencil, rubber and scorebook, I felt sympathy for Don Quixote contemplating his windmills: 'unentreverado loco, lleno de lucidos intervalo . . . *a muddled fool, full of lucid intervals!*

During cricket matches in South America, the first problem I found was to discover an opposition scorer versed in Spanish semaphore. In Belgrano the umpire consistently counted five ball overs because: 'The chap the other end was giving seven balls!'

At Hurlingham, a gust of wind dislodged gallons of water, soaking the Troubadours' scorebook.

In Barretos, Brazil, 10-year-old Sam Wellington took over the scorebook and produced a beautiful Portuguese hierogram.

It was thanks to Argentine beef that our team had sufficient muscle to lift up a stationary car blocking our bus on the road to the Sao Paulo Athletic Club, and deposit it on the pavement.

We approached Barretos after seven hours bussing from Sao Paolo, through forest, sugar cane fazendas, and orange tree plantations.

The sports ground adjoins the Vestey's abattoir, where 1200 cattle are slaughtered daily.

This is a place where nothing is done in halves.

Hot Gospel singers serenaded us as we boarded our bus from the hotel.

Tractors transported ice to the pavilion.

Steaks like flying saucers were grilled on the barbecue for morning snacks.

Cricket, however, was the prelude to the real match of the day, rugby water polo, where the result was a half drowned scorer.

In Brazil cork matting reinforces the cricket pitch, and under the matting a mixture of sand and soil can deflect or neutralise the bounce of the ball, and produce unexpected turns and twists for the bowler. This is the land of not so much yorkers, but corkers!

And talking about Yorkers, we were delighted at Buenos Aires airport to meet up with Susan Barrantes. We look forward in some future year to playing at Trenque Lauquen, with a team perhaps augmented by a prince or two . . .

The Troubadours played seven games in Argentina, and three in Brazil, winning eight, drawing one and losing one. Injuries such as twisted ankles and mosquito bites, induced the scorer to join the field, and this added to his memories of an unforgettable tour.'

TWENTY-TWO

- India -

ARMY LIFE PROVIDED THE OPPORTUNITY and fascination for travel, for reaching those known and obscure blobs on the atlas, and exploring the diversities of geography and the human race. Discarding the uniform for slacks and hats-floppy, for the next 37 years I had the wonderful opportunity of trekking, motoring and boating around Egypt, Kashmir, India and Burma, Thailand, Sri Lanka, South Africa and China, Viet Nam, Sumatra and Gomera, and the Dominican Republic - to name but a few of my many exotic destinations.

India's infamous Black Hole of Calcutta was the guard room in the old Fort William there, where on 19 June 1756 the Nawab of Bengal laid siege to the fort, and 146 British and Anglo-Indian prisoners were pushed into the guard room, where in the unimaginable heat they *raved, fought, prayed, blasphemed, and fell exhausted, where suffocation put an end to their torments.*

Nearby, in happier times, I watched a thousand children and adults playing cricket on the Maidan, a huge expanse of green outside Fort William, doubtless aspiring to emulate their cricketing heroes, Prince Ranjitsinghjis and Tendulkar.

Varanasi, on the Ganges, is a centre of learning for Sanskrit scholars, near where the Buddha first preached his message of enlightenment. For Hindus it is an auspicious place to die, giving an instant route to heaven. I watched the burning ghats, the cremation of the bodies, and the remains swathed in white cloths being carried down to the Ganges on bamboo stretchers.

Eighty-four kilometres from Udaipur lies the impressive 15th century fortress of Kumbhalgarth with its 12 kilometres of walls, on top of the Aravalli range at 1100 metres. It once took the combined armies of the Moghul emperor, Akbar, to breach its defences.

I wandered around its 360 temples of Kumhalgarth, and was reminded of the story of the early pilgrim who beseeched the Maharajah to behead him, the pilgrim, and build a temple and a great wall wherever his head and body fell.

The backwaters of Kerala comprise a complex network of lagoons, rivers and canals.

Travelling there, in style, on a rice boat, one passes traditional craft with huge sails and prows carved into the shape of dragons. Sadly, with illegal land reclamation, urban development, dynamite and poison fishing, and the choking spread of water hyacinths, the area of the lakes is drastically receding, but it is still a truly beautiful area.

Visiting romantic Mankotta Island, with its thousands of farmed ducks patrolled from river to lake, it was not surprising to find on our Indian hosts' menu that evening 'Mankotta Duck!'

In Western Sikkim, at the base of the 2085 metres Kanchenjunga, there stands Pemayangtse (Perfect Sublime Lotus) - an old and important monastery, founded in 1705.

The 'Captain', Yapo Yongda, offered me a room in the Buddhist meditation centre by the monastery, and showed me around the orphanage, where I saw the children chanting and studying, and listened with delight to their song of welcome.

They rise every morning at 4.30 for prayer and work.

Yaro was intrigued to hear that in England I was a school governor, and asked me to address the 250 children at Assembly in the forecourt next morning.

My greetings to them were duly translated!

I travelled down the Irrawaddy from Mandalay in a riverboat full of families, goats and sheep . . .

On Mt Pangulubaum, in Sumatra, I hunted wild orchids, and in Bukit – orangutan.

Debbie Emerson, snapped while out shopping at Ko Pha Ngan, Thailand

Some of the children at Pemayangste Orphanage, Sikkim

Asian cock-fighting

Brother Seymour, his wife Tricia and author paddling around Mankotta Island,

I was very moved by the dedication the priests gave to these 'underprivileged, disadvantaged and destitute children'.

North East of Kashmir lies the remote Tibetan plateau region, known as Ladakh.

The long road from Leh to Manali, rising to 5328 metres, is the most terrifying and dangerous road I have ever encountered, with its rock falls, vehicles hanging over precipices, ice and snow, potholes, craters and collapsed roads.

The war between India and Pakistan, over Kashmir, has produced misery and tension, with the army camping in the villages, and their vehicles clogging the roads.

Away in the country, in Tsomoriri, at 4,500 metres is the home of snow leopards, grey wolf and gazelle, Himalayan marmot, and black necked crane.

Nomadic herders from Tibet sell their pashmina goat wool in the markets there, where I bought scarves for my two nieces, Sophie and Georgie.

In war-ravaged Sri Lanka I was twice to see Chaminda Suranjith, a child I had sponsored through 'Save the Children'. I went to his humble home in Colombo where I met his sister, aunt and granny. With an interpreter to help me I took the children out to lunch, which turned out to be the first time in their lives they had ever eaten in a restaurant.

No visit to Sri Lanka would be complete without visiting Kandy, the capital of the last Sinhalese kingdom, which for three centuries had warded off the Portugese and Dutch – finally succumbing to the British, in 1815.

Finishing the incredible train ride to Kandy, I taxied to the Dalada Maligawa where I saw the sacred tooth of the Buddha, which reputedly had been snatched from the flames of his funeral pyre in 543 BC, and smuggled into Ceylon hidden in the hair of a princess.

In Sumatra, on Mount Pangulubaum, I hunted out wild orchids - and in Bukit Lawang, the orangutan.

In Northern Thailand I stayed with the Hill Tribes, the 'Cho Khao', who invited me to share their opium pipes - and women.

In Burma, for 24-hours I travelled down the River Irrawaddy from Mandalay, in a riverboat full of families, goats and sheep - to Pagan, where my tuk-tuk driver had a degree in economics.

Pagan must be the most amazing sight in all of Burma, with its hundreds of pagodas and temples, built between 1057 and 1287 AD and then abandoned.

In Vietnam I entered the Cu Chi tunnels, built in 1940 against the French. Impervious to bombing, they stretched for 200 kilometres and were several stories deep, with underwater entrances, air vents and living areas, weapons factories, field hospitals and kitchens, and command centres.

By 1966 the Americans had 385,000 servicemen in Vietnam, of which 58,000 would die.

Seeing the craters and leafless trees was evidence of the constant bombing and spraying that was done by US aircraft during that terrible war.

I attended a religious service in the Caudai Great Temple, in Tat Ninh. The Coa Dai religion is a potpourri of Buddhism, Confusionism and Toaism, Hinduism, Spiritualism and Christianity - and Islam. The temple itself is a blend of a French church, a Chinese pagoda, Tiger Balm Gardens and Madame Tussaud's Waxworks, but the service was dignified and impressive.

Trickiest moments in my travels?

Having my hold-all slashed on the Bombay underground, and losing my air tickets.

Being drugged on a Thai bus, and losing my passport.

My travel companions?

Dido - who broke my heart in India.

Deb - who restored it a hundred times with love.

And Seymour, Tricia and Deb braving it in Kerala and Tamil Nadu.

TWENTY-THREE

- A political animal -

IN 1985 I BECAME INVOLVED in local Tory Party politics.

David Mellor was MP for Putney, becoming a privy councillor in 1990, but then falling from grace two years later in scandals involving Max Clifford, Antonia de Sancha's toes, and free holidays with the daughter of a PLO official.

At times it was difficult for any guest speaker in Putney to take the floor after David Mellor's brilliantly witty and powerful introduction, so his self inflicted demise was sad.

The name 'Tory' was originally a disparaging term for an Irish bandit.

For years our headquarters and office in Putney was in Disraeli Road, before moving to Balham.

Politics are 'embedded' in Putney.

In 1647 the famous Putney Debates took place in St Mary's Church, by Putney Bridge, written by a group of civilian Levellers and presided over by Oliver Cromwell. These debates proposed a new Constitution for the country, and rights for the people.

For the last 25 years my pivotal role in the Putney Conservative Association has been to assist in the drive for cash, by organising and attending branch drink parties, wine tasting events and barbecues, scrabble evenings and political dinners.

Political parties are behemoths, with an insatiable appetite for money.

In spite of receiving some huge donations, some from dubious deals with Arabs and others, the party still exerts a relentless pressure on its branches for even more and more money.

At times of election for the European and Westminster Parliaments, or for the London Assembly and local government, we committee members go out to chat up house owners, push thousands of letters and pamphlets though ill-fitting letter boxes, get attacked by savage house dogs and parrots, and endure doorstep diatribes from 'fed up housewives'.

Besides 'Knocking Up' at elections, we 'tell' outside polling booths, ticking off the faithful Tory voters so they won't be bothered by 'knockers up' later in the day.

On many occasions I have accompanied our MP or councillors, and have noted householders' opinions on noisy low flying aircraft, dog messes, cyclists on pavements, foxes raiding dustbins and rowdy revellers at pub closing hours.

Our branch of the Putney Conservative Association is Thamesfield, with Justine Greening as our current Member of Parliament.

An independent think-tank voted Justine, a Yorkshire lass, as the ninth best value for money MP.

She is now Economic Secretary to the Treasury, and with myself is a Deputy Chair of Governors at Hotham Primary School.

Our local councillor is Edward Lister, who is also Leader of Wandsworth Council. Eddie runs a very successful council, but infuriated many voters in Putney by selling off the one and only local market garden site, and attempting to sell the Sea Scouts' premises on the river.

With a present hung parliament (2010), a Conservative Liberal coalition and David Cameron slashing government spending, I have now taken a back seat in local politics, resigning from the Thamesfield committee, but continuing to organise and run the popular scrabble evenings at the local Putney Tandoori, owned by avid Tory supporter, Mr Ahmed, from Bangladesh.

TWENTY-FOUR

- *Academe* -

IN 1990 I WAS APPOINTED a governor of Hotham Primary School, Putney.

School governors are appointed from parents, the community, teaching staff, and the London Education Authority – who was my own appointee.

Each governor is a member of one of four committees: either Curriculum, Premises, Finance or Executive. My own committee is Premises, in which we deliberate and decide on capital works, energy and water, lettings, cleaning contracts, health and safety, decorating, security, heating, fire alarms and playgrounds and gardens.

Hotham School took its name from Admiral William Hotham, a brother officer of Horatio Nelson.

It was founded in 1909, with 600 pupils.

Hotham Road was part of the Putney Velodrome Estate, where the world cycling and walking events took place from 1891 to 1905, watched at the time by no fewer than 10,000 spectators.

In 1729 Parliament granted permission for a Thames bridge to be built at Putney - the only bridge between Kingston and London Bridge.

And prior to that, between AD 43 and 410, along the Thames the Putney embankment had been a busy thoroughfare for the Romans, too.

So Hotham School is strategically and historically well placed!

In 1909 boys and girls were kept apart, having separate staircases and playgrounds.

The poorer children were given clothes by the better-off families.

The council inspectors once had occasion to report: *Unpunctuality is almost unknown in the senior departments,* and *The ball carpet for dancing is worthy of special mention.*

In 1935 Hotham had a dizzying 1,124 pupils on its roll. The poorest children in the school were provided with lunch for one penny, and made their way to a local coffee shop, but then in the early 1970s Hotham built its own kitchens.

In 1913 the playground was used for drilling the National Reserve. Ten school staff members went off to fight, and all of them safely returned.

In 1919 each pupil was given a plate and a mug to celebrate 'the Great Victory of the British Empire'.

In 1940, in common with 600,000 other London school children, Hotham pupils were evacuated, to avoid the bombing raids. Tearfully leaving behind their distraught parents they were given a bag, with a gas mask, some clothes and a label pinned to their coats, showing their name and school, and sent by train to various safer corners of England.

In 1990, as a governor I became heavily involved in a scheme to rebuild an Edwardian pavilion in the school grounds.

This pavilion had been used to teach children with tuberculosis, who were thought to need fresh air.

Fortuitously, we had amongst our governors an architect, Alison Lowe, who designed and supervised the new project.

First we cajoled funds from banks, supermarkets and charities, and then appointed a professional, Gwyn Jones, to design and create a 'Secret Garden' with a human sundial, mirror mosaic, trickle fountain, geological pavement and Spring, Summer and Autumn gardens.

Hotham School today has 333 pupils, aged from 3 to 11 years old, and is ranked 'outstanding' by Ofsted.

Thirty-three per cent of the children are white British, and the remainder were born in Bangladesh, Nigeria and the West Indies, Somaliland, South America and China, India, Pakistan and Eastern Europe. Our head teacher, Pam Young, is Hong Kong Chinese from New Zealand.

Currently the school is undergoing a massive restructuring programme of enlargement, and in 2011 will become bi-lingual in English and French.

TWENTY-FIVE

- Anchors aweigh -

IN NOVEMBER 1997 I ENLISTED as a crew member on board the Sail Training Association's Tall Ship *Sir Winston Churchill*.

We joined the ship in Lisbon, Portugal, and after 928 nautical miles, 136 hours at sea, and an average speed of 6.8 knots, arrived in the Canaries.

Our skipper was Hugh O'Neill.

We had a chief officer, bosun, engineer and cook, navigator, purser, and three 'watches' of 14 crew members.

In all weathers and at all hours we climbed the rat-lines, set the 45 metre top gallant and royal sails, braced the yards, handed the mizzen, hoisted the topsail - and took turns peeling spuds in the galley.

On returning to dry land a chance meeting with Michael Prest, Chairman of the STA London Committee, persuaded me to join his board.

My enthusiasm for the organisation undaunted, I set about learning a little of its past.

The Sail Training Association (STA) was formed in 1956, when Royal Navy cadets took part in the first European Tall Ships Race, from Torbay to Lisbon, on the yacht *Creole*, lent to them by Stavros Niarchos.

The STA commissioned the UK's first Tall Ship *Sir Winston Churchill*, and shortly afterwards *The Malcolm Miller* through the generosity of the Lord Mayor of London, Sir James Miller.

By the mid 1990s these two schooners had taken 40,000 young people to sea in fortnightly voyages across the oceans and in series of European Tall Ship races.

Whilst attending London committee meetings, cajoling the 16 – 24-year-old youths in London youth clubs and schools to sail with the Association, fundraising, and manning the STA stands at the Earls Court Boat Show, I decided to continue active participation with the Tall Ships.

I joined *The Malcolm Miller* for another memorable voyage from Lisbon to the Canaries, this time in force 7/8 gales.

In following years I joined the Tall Ships sailing around the Canaries.

On one occasion, to the astonishment of the local community and tourists, we had two pipers on board who led our happily smiling crew through the streets of Tenerife.

On another occasion a midwife on my watch climbed into my bunk, because: 'I felt too ill to climb up to my own'!

In 2000 two new brigs were commissioned, the *Stavros Niarchos* and the *Prince William,* to replace our elderly schooners, and in that year I sailed on the *Stavros Niarchos'* maiden voyage from Gibraltar to Tenerife.

For shore leave we anchored off Essaouira 'the most enchanting town on the coast of Morocco'.

In 1760 the Sultan used his captive French architect to design the walls and Medina to good effect.

At departure time a large swell necessitated us having to use the RIBS to carry us back with some difficulty to the *Niarchos.*

In 2003 the STA became the Tall Ships Youth Trust.

By 2005, 3,000 people were sailing in the schooners each year.

In 2007 the Trust decided to remove *Prince William* from operation, and purchase six *Challenger* class yachts, to provide a wider choice of sailing.

I recently joined a *Challenger* in the Azores, with six Azores sea scouts as crew. In very rough weather they were all seasick, so we remaining six crew worked overtime!

I am now Chairman of the Tall Ships Youth Trust, South West London.

The widespread use of computers has enabled young people to log on and book direct with the Trust.

I give advice on line, and talk to London schools about all the character-building adventure and excitement that is derived from sailing in our Tall Ships.

On board a Challenger off the Azores; It was such rough weather that the Sea Scouts were all sick.

On Tall Ship *Sir Winston Churchill;* we clambered up the rat lines at all hours in all weathers . . .

Brothers in Arms - Reunited: my brother Seymour Gilbart-Denham and I visit our father's wartime grave at Harstadt, Norway - 1998

Robert Corbett and Sgt Boyd at Colenso (Irish Guards Centenary Boer War Battlefield Tour 2000)

TWENTY-SIX

-Gravely nostalgic -

IN JUNE 1998 MY BROTHER Seymour and I decided to visit our father's war time grave, in Norway.

The background to this visit I wrote about shortly afterwards in the *Guards Magazine.*

Here it is:-

On 30th November 1939, Russia attacked Finland on her southern borders.

The British Chiefs of Staff were authorised to *plan for a landing force at Narvik, for the sake of Finland, and for a possible German occupation of Southern Norway.*

On 15th April the Irish Guards landed unopposed in Harstadt, high up in the Arctic Circle.

Six days previously, seven German and Austrian divisions, 800 operational aircraft and 300 transport planes had invaded the 1,700 mile length of Norway.

A British flotilla, under Captain Warburton-Lee, RN, then gallantly destroyed most of the German ships in Narvik's harbour.

The arrival of 24th Guards Brigade was followed by three battalions of Chasseurs Alpin, two French Foreign Legion battalions, and the Polish Highland Brigade.

After enduring a week of relentless bombing, the Irish Guards moved out of Harstadt to take up positions around Bogen Bay, in preparation for an assault on Narvik.

My father, Vivian, in heavily censored letters, described his situation:

It has snowed without stopping for seven days . . . Of course all transport for baggage is by sledge . . . The scenery is just too wonderful to describe. Not a ripple on the water and lovely snow-clad mountains reflect in the still waters, with here and there duck and wild geese floating gracefully by . . . The worst thing is the absence of any form of bath. I have yet to find out how the natives manage to look so clean!

Norway had a population of 2 ½ million, and an army of 7,000 soldiers with no sub machine-guns, no anti-aircraft guns, and no tanks.

Their Admiral had described his Navy as 'My old bath tubs'.

Norway tried to remain neutral, but it was not to be.

After 14 days fighting, and being harassed by continual bombing and gunning from the air, the heroic Norwegian troops were exhausted.

Notices on their walls pronounced:

The greatest warmonger of this century, Mr Churchill, has prepared the attack on the Norwegian coast - Every citizen caught with weapons in hand will be SHOT.

Meantime, as Harstadt flamed, the Irish Guards surveyed the Narvik shoreline and prepared for assault.

Their anxious thoughts can be imagined.

One-hundred-and-sixty-years previously, British soldiers storming the fort of Seringapatam were nicknamed the Forlorn Hopes. Sergeants who survived were promised a commission, and all ranks a purse of gold.

The Irish Guards never did storm Narvik's Vassvika pier. The Guardsmen never got their purse of gold. Appalling weather caused the postponement of the operation, and the capture of Narvik was to be left to the French and the Poles.

The Irish Guards battalion was embarked on a comfortable new Polish cruise ship, the *Chrobry,* with orders to reinforce the beleaguered Allied troops at Mo, south of Narvik.

They never got to Mo.

In the clear midnight sun three Heinkels dropped their bombs amidships on the *Chrobry.*

A Sub-Lieutenant Dalzel-Job had for safety reasons argued energetically for the use of his puffer fleet for the transport of the Irish Guards to Mo and Bodo, but had been briskly overruled by command in Harstad, in spite of support from their C-in-C, Lieutenant Colonel Faulkner.

Now the bombs cut through the flimsy roofs of the top cabins, occupied by the senior officers, ultimately killing the commanding officer, second in command, adjutant and the three most senior company commanders.

694 Guardsmen were evacuated in 16 minutes by the escort naval craft, *Stock* and *Wolverine.*

Commander Crane, RN, was later to report: *Their conduct in the most terrifying circumstances, in the absence of senior officers, on a burning and sinking ship, open at any time to a new attack, was as fine as, or finer than, the conduct in the old days of the soldiers on the* Birkenhead.

Seymour and I visited the locations in Bogen Bay where in 1940 the Irish companies had been deployed.

We travelled on the Ofoten railway from Narvik in Norway to Lulea in Sweden.

Locomotives on this line ferried iron ore from Sweden, essential for the German arms industry in the Ruhr, which was the major reason for the British decision to capture Narvik.

Like so many railways, from India to Argentine, it was built by the British, a major feat of engineering comprising numerous bridges and tunnels.

In Harstadt, we located our father's grave.

A photograph of us beside the grave was taken by Elen Trolic, who had managed to escape up into the hills with her sister and baby brother in 1940, when the Germans invaded.

Five years later, in 2003, I was to organise a remembrance tour of the Narvik region, with Irish Guards veterans and relations, together with Antony Shaw, the historian, whose grandfather was on *Chrobry,* Major Leslie Upton, who at the time was RASC clerk to the Commander of 24 Guards Brigade, ex-Scots Guardsman Rollings, and - most importantly - Judith Richardson-Chapple, our Norwegian speaking tour leader from Putney!

On arrival we had a fascinating talk at the Narvik museum, a tour of the fiords and of the Bogen Bay area, and a drive and exploration of the *Sami* Museum, to learn about those indigenous Norwegians in the northern Arctic.

Douglas Scott talked in the Narvik cemetery to the group about his father, Colonel Montagu-Douglas-Scott, and his uncle, Lt-Col W.D.Faulkner, who commanded the battalion in Norway, and was killed on the *Chrobry.*

The highlight of the tour was our group embarking on the Norwegian Navy's *stridsbaten* (fast patrol boats) and laying a wreath in the *Tjeldsundet* sea near the spot where the *Chrobry* was bombed by the German Heinkels.

In Harstadt the Mayor and Corporation lunched us in style.

After presentations by both sides, I replied in Norwegian (thanks to Judith, our tour leader!):-

Thank you Mr Mayor for the great reception you have given us today in Harstadt. Sixty-three years ago men from 24 Guards Brigade landed here, three of whom are here with us today. Many were hospitalised here. Some with local girls fell in love here. Some died here. The German wireless announced that the (British) landing had been made by 'hired volunteers and unemployed'. And the peace that Harstadt had known for a hundred years was shattered, as the city was bombed and battered to ruins. But what a magnificent and proud city you now have! Very many thanks from us all for your welcome.

TWENTY-SEVEN

- *These boots are meant for walking* -

THE SOUTH WEST COASTAL PATH measures 630 miles, and stretches from Minehead in Somerset, through north Devon and Cornwall, to Haven Point in South Dorset.

Its total ascent and descent is 35,030 metres, four times the height of Everest from sea level!

The most strenuous parts of the path are from Lynmouth to Coombe Martin (1350 metres) and Hartland Bay to Bude Canal (1302 metres).

Over a decade I have walked the entire path, carrying my rucksack, and armed with a walking pole to ward off adders, nettles and ferocious highland cattle!

My walks are planned under the working title *Operation Claudius,* so named after legions of the Roman Emperor Claudius, who established a fort in Isca Dumnoniorum (Exeter) and made expeditions into Cornwall, principally to collect tin from the mines on the North coast.

Around about the first century BC, the Greek historian Diodorus Siculus described tin mining in Cornwall, thus: *These are the people who prepare the tin and mix it with some veins of earth, out of which they melt the metal and refine it.*

On average I covered about 12 miles a day, walking at two mph. My accommodation at B & Bs was pre-booked, and varied in quality and price, with space not always reflecting the description of a single or double room.

In Charlestown once, my landlady was so horrified by my soaked appearance after walking in six hours of solid rain, that she hesitated to let me in. However, having shed my sodden boots and soaking clothes in her hall, by the time I had stripped to my dripping underpants, I had won her over.

On every occasion, I found landladies provided a gargantuan breakfast of bacon, eggs and sausages, black pudding, tomatoes and baked beans, potato cakes and toast.

The coastline always provided a panorama of sights and views.

I have seen board surfing in pounding seas, seals and sharks; white horses thrashing into copper stained rocks, sandy beaches and smugglers' coves, and then derelict tin mines at Botallack.

Every mile of every trip offered different interests: the Minack Theatre on the cliffs at Porthcurno; the wireless station at Poldhu, where in 1901 the 27-year-old Guglielmo Marconi transmitted the first wireless Morse signals to St John's, in Newfoundland; the Rev Robert Hawker's hut in Morwenstow, where he smoked opium and prepared sermons admonishing the Morwenstow wreckers for *allowing a fainting brother to perish in the sea without extending a hand of safety.*

Then there was the Swannery, at Abbotsbury, established by Benedictine monks in 1040; or, on the Lizard, the serpentine and granite church of St Winwallow, Landewednack, with its lepers' windows, derived from 'Lezard' - the old term for Leper.

At Tintagel, Debbie Emerson and I unknowingly were invited to attend a Scientology 'dreamland' induction at the Camelot Castle Hotel, and declined.

Along the Helford passage, Cherry Crawford slipped and became a mud lark.

At Portwrinkle, tempers frayed when Meriel Larken and I became separated.

At Port Quin, a dog joined us, walking for miles and refusing to leave.

At Lyme Regis, on the Jurassic coast, rock falls led to confusing diversions in the forested hills above.

Around Lulworth, where their training area lies, we were obliged to dodge the Army's tanks, guns and bullets.

And additional rewards there were aplenty: the world's largest greenhouse, the Eden Project, just off the path at St Austell, for example.

Rick Stein's restaurants and sea bars at Padstow.

The National Trust's Glendurgan Gardens at Mawnan Smith, the Trengwainton Gardens at Penzance - and St Michael's Mount.

Dining in the pubs of Looe, Polperro and Mevagissey, Coverack, Lamorna and Mousehole on Cornwall's south coast, I saw in the old photographs on the walls constant reminders of smuggling in the 18th and 19th centuries, when tea, brandy and rum was dropped off in sheltered coves and tunnels, and passages dug out of the rocks - smugglers who when caught were hanged or transported, like Robert Lang, from Veryan, who was hanged at the crossroads of Ruanlanihorne and St Mawes.

Along the coastal path often I passed huers' huts.

The observant huer would alert his colleagues by crying out 'Hevva' through a trumpet whenever he sited the massive shoals of pilchard. Using semaphore he would then guide the boats to the shoal, and huge nets, 400 yards in length, would be thrown around them. The pilchards, whose by-product, oil, was used for lighting and heating, were highly prized and exported far and wide.

Two-thousand-years ago the Romans dumped their convicts on the Isles of Scilly, which is why, following the steps of Claudius, Deb and I flew there by helicopter. (No – he went by boat).

We stayed at St Mary's, then boated to Tresco to see the semi-tropical Abbey Gardens: there was not much sign of the Romans, or the convicts, but we did discover gooseberry ice cream, which like a ride in a helicopter, Claudius and his legions would never have got to taste either.

TWENTY-EIGHT

- Roof of the world -

In a thousand ages of the gods I could not tell thee
Of the glories of the Himalaya; just as the dew is dried
By the morning sun, so are the sins of humankind
By the sight of the Himalaya

Skanda Purana

KATHMANDU.

Tuesday 27th March, 2007.

My cousin, John Royden, had organised an international group of ten to go out to trek and climb in the Himalayas.

The four amongst us attempting to scale the 8,840 metre-high summit of Everest itself, were Ben Stephens, Tori James, from Wales, Greg Maud, from South Africa, and Omar Samra, from Egypt.

Those of our six trekkers content just to head for Everest Base Camp, at a mere 5,360 metres, were my cousin, John Royden - and Biril Raja, who originally came from India; also from the same Egyptian womb, Omar Samra's brother, Ahmed - Fiona Wrench, from South Africa, Sophie Bainbridge, from darkest Oxfordshire - and the idiotic 72-year-old Brian Gilbart-Denham, from Putney.

Originally classified as Peak XV, the greatest mountain in the world became named after the Welsh-born surveyor/geographer, Col Sir George Everest (1790-1866), who was Britain's Surveyor General in India between 1830-43.

At the time of writing, there have been over 4, 000 ascents of Everest.

Above the 8,000 metre 'death zone' (beyond which many don't proceed farther) there still lie at least 150 unrecovered 'stiffs'.

Altitude sickness, which is caused by low blood-oxygen vastly increasing one's breathing rate, is the greatest health hazard.

Avalanches are the greatest climbing hazard.

The black jumping spider, the highest non-microscopic permanent resident on earth, the bar-headed goose - and the chough, these would be our companions.

Wednesday 28th March.

The team flew from Kathmandu, in a small 16-seater plane, to Lukla (2886 metres), landing on a strip 100 metres long, and then de-planed to start hacking into the mountainside at a frightening 15 degrees – the commencement of our journey to Everest Base Camp.

We would be climbing for about six hours a day, resting and eating in huts along the route.

Huts on the lower slopes there were aplenty, but higher than 4,000 metres they were few and far between.

Comfort in these basic abodes was Spartan, but adequate.

A shower, costing a few rupees, would be available, with hot water being poured into a tank by a helpful Sherpa.

Garlic soup followed by yak meat and apple pie were our menus' tantalising items.

Stoves burning yak dung provided heat during the night – as well as suffocating fumes.

Wearing a head torch at night was strongly advised, for those of us who might need to negotiate the strewn piles of yak dung in order to reach the DTLs (deep trench latrines).

Early reveille was no problem, because the morning sun would melt the ice on the corrugated tin roof, and water dripped down onto our bunks.

From Lukla we then trekked to Namche Bazar.

Namshe Bazar (3,440 metres) is the main trading village in the Khumbu region, the resting place for travellers heading north. It is a town bustling with shops, vendors and traders, great food, and fantastic views of Mount Everest itself, and Lhotse, which is the fourth highest peak in the world.

We stopped there for two nights, before heading for Dole, passing stupas (mound-like structures containing Buddhist relics), prayer flags, Mani stones and prayer wheels.

My blog - transmitted to the wide world by satellite - described our Cho Oyu Lodge, Dole (4,040 metres) daily routine thus:-

0645   Reveille
0730   Breakfast: Honey pancakes, dodging socks marinating over the stove, fill up water for the CamelBaks, and of course 'No Smoking in the Dinning'.
0745   Sophie's group therapy and stretching exercises. Porters: LakBahandu Hatri, Rakh Kobir Ri, Rad Touri Ri, Ankham Mi Cherpa, Mohar Bahain Katri, Dinek Nethri get the baggage together. 'We must take a monk with us next time,' says John. 'With prayer wheels,' says Brian.
0815   Set off. SNOMP - snow, mud and puddles. Roads have given way to tracks.
1030   Hangteva Lodge. Barren landscape, tufts of heather, cold wind.
1145   Tashi Dele Lodge 4392m, 23 km from Lukla. Night stop. Tori and Greg set up satellite communications, Biral sets up his hammock (a public erection).
1330   Lunch

By now we were becoming pretty much acclimatised and learning the rhythm of walking, and the ways of the yaks, charging like T54 tanks along the tracks, heavily loaded, whipped and encouraged by their drivers, oblivious to anyone or thing in their path.

When we stopped for rests Ben would insist on us, his flock, imbibing pints of water, while Tori stressed upon us the importance of proper breathing.

Biral would sing, and sometimes discard his clothing to lie spread eagled in the snow.

John would be considering further brain aching variations of the card game 'Hearts' which he could inflict on his comrades.

Sophie provided the cabaret, by cracking the floorboards of a DTL (latrine) and nearly falling down the bottomless pit to Hades.

By Tuesday 3rd April we had reached Gokyo, and at 3.00 next morning, in freezing weather, climbed to the top of Gokyu Ri (5,480 metres) to catch the first rays of sunshine as they lit the summit of Cho Oyu, a short way to our north.

Fiona led our rendition of 'Happy Birthday' to Greg, as a prelude to presenting him with a squashed Caramello Bear.

Sophie wrote: *Around 5.a.m. the sky began to lighten, silhouetting these peaks (Everest, Lhotse, Nuptse, Makalu) against the dawn horizon. It was without doubt one of the most spectacular sights I've seen.*

From there we trekked to the Ngozumpa Glacier and the 5,330 metre Cho La Pass.

My blog, by satellite to the world, described it:-

0415   Reveille
0445   Baggage ready for porters
0500   Breakfast: Pancakes with eggs, chapatti, jam, Tibetan bread. General Ben, like Henry V before the Battle of Agincourt, addresses his troops. 'Your oxygen now is 50% that of sea level. Take a breath now with each step'.
0535   The team starts to traverse the Cho La Pass, a distance of 7½ km, and 8½ hours trekking. The ground resembles Dartmoor, with boulders, and rocks, black, grey, green, ochre, copper, silver, gold and bronze, and

speckled with lichen and moss. Fiona's fingers are frozen, Ben has a splitting headache, and skirted like that indomitable Victorian traveler Hester Stanhope, Sophie draws admiring glances from grazing yaks. Climbing steadily up the moraine towards the top of the Cho La Pass at an angle of 35 degrees, Ben produces his ice pick to carve steps in the iced packed snow.

1205   5,330m, the top! Greg leads Brian, who will miss the delights of Everest Base Camp, to a small peak 5376m and 9m above the height of Base Camp.

We next made a log traverse to the Ngozumpa Glacier, and then on to the Summer Yak Herding Station at Dzonglha (4,830 metres), where we spent an uncomfortable cold night wrapped in thermal socks and underwear, woolly hats and gloves, inhaling yellow yak dung smoke and listening to scratching rats.

At Gorak Shep (5,160 metres) we were reunited with Omar and his brother, Ahmed, last seen at Namshe, where Omar had been taken ill.

Emotionally, I left the group at Gorak Shep, and with a Sherpa guide trekked at speed through Namche, to Lukla, for a flight to Khatmandu back to London to attend my niece, Sophie's, all important wedding to Ollie Mudie.

After a series of adventures Ben, Tori, Greg and Omar, did reach the summit of Mount Everest.

Omar, the first Egyptian to do so, proudly planted his national flag, and Tori, the youngest Welsh woman, proudly planted the Welsh flag.

All of them descended safely.

TWENTY-NINE

- A glutton for punishment -

AFTER OUR GREAT TRIP to Everest Base Camp, the following year John Royden and I, accompanied by an American rugby- playing lawyer friend of ours, Carey Depel, decided to climb Mont Blanc (4,810 metres) - *La Dame Blanche* - the highest mountain in the Alps.

Mont Blanc attracts thousands of climbers each year, and also accounts for hundreds of casualties.

It is considered to be the most dangerous mountain in the world, notorious for avalanches.

It can also be a very cold mountain: in January 1893 a temperature of -43C degrees was recorded.

In 2007 a group of 20 climbers enterprisingly set up a hot tub at the summit of Mont Blanc, but John, Carey and I thought that we would still prefer to take our baths at our base, in Chamonix.

We arrived at Chamonix on Saturday 14th June 2008, in the worst weather conditions for 40 years.

For six weeks there had been continuous rain and sleet in the town, and snow in the mountains.

Our principal guides for the next few weeks would be Guy Willet, a qualified climber, doctor and geologist, and the appropriately named Kenton Cool, who with six successful Everest ascents behind him was probably Britain's top mountain guide.

Over the next three days we practised the use of crampons, ice picks and ropes, trekked in deep snow from L'Aiguille du Midi, the mountain cable car stop, to the Tête Rousse Cabin, where we stayed the night, midst the snoring and snorting of 70 other climbers.

On our return we held a Council of War with Guy, and collectively decided to abort the climb, because of the deep, unstable snow and potential dangers of rock falls and avalanches.

We would move over to Italy instead, there to attempt the 4,061 metres Massif of the Gran Paradiso.

My diary recorded:-

Wed 18 Jun   Drove two hours into Italy
Thu 19 Jun   0350 hrs Reveille
0445 hrs Start off with headlamps
0545 hrs Stop to fix on crampons and rope
0900 hrs Kenton received news from Mt Blanc that a Swiss guide and 5 climbers had been swept to their deaths, and two badly injured air lifted.
1145 hrs summit reached.

I was roped to Dave, an expert Australian mountaineer.

In spite of wearing two pairs of gloves, my fingers were frozen to the bone.

The ascent was steep towards the summit, with deep snow and howling wind.

The rope tightened as Dave hauled me up, and I could now see, right at the top, a statue of the Madonna.

Then ropes were secured to me fore and aft, and I traversed my way around a rock for 7-metres on a 4in ledge, and then inched my way for 10-metres along an 8in knife-edge ridge, trying not to look down on the sheer drops on either side.

I could see a Spanish team grouped around the Madonna, praying.

Carey had clipped his gaiters on a rock, and was unsteady.

Kenton was swearing, 'We cannot fall off this f*****g summit, even my sister can do f*****g better than this!'

After first reaching out and touching the Madonna, I inched back along the ledges, roped again on to Dave, and we were slowly able to make our way to the Refuge (at 2,732 metres) for a welcome coke.

Some of the Spanish team, obviously amazed that a veteran had survived the ordeal, came to offer me their salami sausages and some encouragement!

We had conquered the Massif!

In 1916 the Italians fought a ferocious war against the Germans and Austrians, in the mountains of the Dolomites. Thousands of troops died of cold, falls or avalanches. Both sides tried to gain control of the peaks, to site their observation posts and field guns. They also tried to create and control tunnels below the peaks, to be able to attack from there. To help troops move about at high altitude, in very difficult conditions, permanent lines were fixed to rock faces, and ladders were installed, so the troops could ascend steep faces. These were the first *vie ferrate* (iron roads). The wartime network of *vie ferrate (*single*: via ferrata)* has since been restored, with new routes added. Steel cables have replaced ropes, and iron ladders and metal rungs (stemples) anchored into the rock have taken the place of the flimsy wooden structures used by the troops.

On Saturday 21st June we drove to Grand Bornand *Via Ferrata* near the Col de la Columbiere, and glanced apprehensively up at its 1,100 metres of cables, stemples, ladders and bridges.

The climb was from 1,400 metres to 2,000 metres, taking about five hours.

We donned our harnesses, two short ropes with attached carabiners, and helmets.

I was attached throughout to Kenton, the leader, who made sure that I clipped my carabiner on to each rung in front of me, and the guy behind me then unclipped it, as we moved forward and up.

I found it terrifying, and tried not to look down as we scaled high and higher, with limbs stretching to breaking point, and fingers and toes feeling for niches in the rocks.

Kenton showed admirable patience, checking my carabiner and directing my hands and feet whilst also taking corroborative digital snapshots of this septuagenarian limpet along the way!

So, we were denied the prize of reaching the pinnacle of *La Dame Blanche,* but we did reach the statue of the Madonna in the Massif of the Gran Paradiso, and we did scale the Grand Bornand *Via Ferrata.* Probably of equal achievement, and certainly more enjoyable!

THIRTY

Himalayas revisited

The Secret of the mountains is that the mountains simply exist,
as I do myself:
The mountains exist simply, which I do not.
The mountains have no 'meaning'; they are meanings;
The mountains are.

Peter Matthiessen
The Snow Leopard

Major Ram Prasad Gurung, came to tea with myself and John Royden, in Putney, in July 2009.

Ram, an ex-Gurkha, owned and managed a trekking company in Nepal.

Midst the sipping of Earl Grey, the seeds were sown for an Annapurna Circuit trek, to take place in March the following year.

In 1950 Annapurna had been the first of the great Himalayan summits of over 8,000 metres to be scaled, by the 30-year-old French mountaineer, Maurice Herzog, who sadly lost most of his toes and fingers in that historic achievement.

On Thursday 25th March 2010, our group met at the Summit Hotel, in Kathmandu: Victor Beamish, a stockbroker from Aberdeen, Daniel Green, a cosmopolitan adventurer, my cousin, John Royden, of Everest fame, myself - and lastly . . . 17-year-old Ruairi Bowen, a choral scholar from Hereford.

Major Ram, hitherto as e-mail elusive as a snow leopard, briefed us on the programme, and distributed sleeping bags and quilted jackets.

Victor's luggage had not arrived yet from Aberdeen, so together from our spares we provided everything for him from underpants to goggles.

Next morning we piled into a bus which for hours bumped and lurched along appalling tracks, occasionally breaking down.

We reached Bhulbhule at dusk, vehicle and passengers crippled, to start an eight hour walk to Jagat early the next morning, a rigorous test of fitness and acclimatisation for all.

I had feared for a dodgy Achilles tendon I'd acquired, but stretching the tendon seemed to cure the pain.

That night our porters pitched the tents, and prepared supper.

So began a different routine of sleeping in tents, packing and unpacking in limited space, the use of head torches again, and getting packed and ready to move at first light.

Soon we appreciated the expertise and endurance of our team of porters.

We trekked through picturesque Tal, Dharapani, Koto and Dharamshala, via mountain forests, past red rhododendron, rivers, tumbling waterfalls and rotating prayer wheels, mindful of our karma the whole way.

We passed stupas representing faith, concentration, mindfulness, perseverance and wisdom.

In further days we reached Koto, then climbed steeply into the restricted area of the Tibetan Nar and Phu valleys.

Animals sheltered on the ground floor of the Nar houses, and above them lived the families.

Tree trunks with notches in them provided ladders to the upper floors.

The heavy loads of the men and women carrying wood and water, were supported by head straps.

Women worked the looms, weaving wool for rugs and blankets.

On the village poles blue, yellow and green prayer flags fluttered with prayers and mantras.

With his telescopic lens Ruairi captured the wild goats in the bare landscape.

Now yaks, rather than ponies, were the beasts of burden - and the weather turned icy cold.

From Kotho we prepared to trek the Kang La Pass, at 5,322 metres.

We passed Nar Base Camp, where nearby, on Kanguru Himal, on 20th October 2006, an expedition had been swept away by an avalanche.

Our gallant porters, carrying 30kg on their backs, lugging our bags, the folding supper table and the portable loo through two metres of soft snow, found the going particularly arduous.

As each step broke the shallow crust of ice, it was an effort to lift one's foot for the next.

All walking rhythm was gone.

And it was bitterly cold.

Yet even in these arctic conditions our Sherpas prepared a hot meal for us, and erected our tents.

That night, in heavy-downed sleeping bags, we slept in all our clothes, including hats and gloves.

The Kang La Pass is spectacular, with great views of Annapurna 11, Gangaapurna and Tilicho.

At rests, Victor regaled us with accounts of his shooting on Scottish moors (and ghillies handcuffed for allegedly poisoning protected birds).

Daniel told of his heroic sallies into Afghanistan, and China, John of saucy jokes and jaunts – and young Ruiari of footballing choristers in Hereford

On reaching Manang, a large town of migrated traders from India, our senior guide found out that our intended route, the Khangsar Pass to Tilich Lake, was impassable. So we decided to change our route, following the Thorong La Pass (5,414 metres), the highest pass in the world, and traversing on through the mountains to Lupra, and then onto a seasoned track to Jomson, where we caught a plane to Pokhara.

Pokhara is a thriving metropolis of fun and relaxation, with a mass of water, the Phewa Lake, being a dominant feature.

Here, after boating, exploring temples and the World Peace Stupa, our party split up: Daniel to wild game parks in Nepal, Ruairi to football in India, and Victor to his Scottish stockbroking, leaving John and myself to fly back to Kathmandu together.

No visit to Kathmandu is complete without a visit to the 12th century royal 'City of Devotees', Bhaktapur, filled with its monuments, palaces and temples, gilded roofs and open courtyards.

I saw the *Bisket Jatra,* the Nepalese New Year celebration, chariots being pulled through the streets, followed by a tug of war.

I missed the *Gal-Jatra,* the Cow Festival, with a boy dressed as a cow, representing families in bereavement.

And I missed the tongue-boring ceremony, when a thin metal spike is thrust through the tongue of devotees by the temple's priest.

But I did see the Royal Bath in Durbar Square, and the last King of Bhaktapur's Big Bell, rung to pay homage to the goddess Taleju.

Hotham Primary School Centenary Celebrations - 2009

Brian and Cherry . . .

Gorek Shep, Everest – 5160m

Summit, Gran Paradiso – Author inching his way along an 8in knife-edge ridge

The Author, breathing a little hard on the Massif di Gran Paradiso – 4061m . . . but still gamely truckin' . . . with (hopefully) a good few miles to go on the clock yet!

. . . PAUSE

Meanwhile, back in the UK . . . a conclusion:

- A day in the Life of Brian -

9 a.m. Piano Accordion

The piano accordion was introduced to the world by Bouton of Paris in 1852, and became originally popularised by Count Guido Pietro Deiro (September 1, 1886 - July 26, 1950), the famous Italian vaudeville star, international recording artist, composer and teacher. He was the first piano-accordionist to appear on big-time vaudeville, records, radio and the screen. Guido usually performed under the stage-name "Deiro". Guido and his younger brother Pietro Deiro (known as "Pietro") were among the highest paid musicians on the vaudeville circuit, and they both did much to introduce and popularise the piano accordion in the early 20th century.

Always having admired and enjoyed the instrument, thinking it would be a bit of a wheeze to do so, in 1985 I started to have piano accordion lessons of my own, with a master piano accordionist, the then 82-year-old Italian maestro - L.O. Anzaghi.

My lessons have now long since ceased, but I do still practise whenever I can, with doors and windows closed, to shut out any complaints, criticism or interference.

The piano accordion is a difficult instrument to play, with a key board for the right hand and buttons for the left hand. But I persevere: it provides a discipline, a challenge and a most enjoyable therapy.

11 a.m. Tennis at Hurlingham

The Hurlingham Club – billed as 'an agreeable country resort' - was founded in 1874, in grounds originally owned by the Bishops of London.

Tennis began to be played there in 1887, with a 'lawn racquet ground', and today there are 45 grass, hard, synthetic, clay and indoor courts.

Hurlingham became, and remained until the Second World War - when the grounds were compulsorily purchased by the London County Council - the headquarters of Polo for the British Empire.

During both World Wars Yeomanry balloon detachments were based at the Club.

Today there are more than 10,000 members and a waiting time of 10 years for all new applicants.

For some years now I have regularly played a kind of tennis there.

Paying the required £1, I join my selected partner, and for the next two hours indulge in what my grandfather, Henry Beaumont, described as 'a bit of Hit and Scream'.

We then repair to the polo bar for a cool Pimms with our chums.

2 p.m. Bridge with Andrew Robson

Originally 'cards' were made for fortune telling and gambling.

In 1432 Saint Barnado warned the 'Faithful' that cards were *invented by the Devil.*

By 1495, Henry VII issued a decree forbidding his servants from playing cards, except during the Christmas Holiday.

The game of Bridge was devised from Russian Whist, called Biritch, meaning an announcer (players 'announce or herald' their auction).

The faces on the *Kings* were based on historical rulers: e.g. **King Clubs** – Alexander the Great.

On the *Queens* the origin is debatable: **Queen Spades** – Pallas warrior goddess (Minerva).

On the *Jacks* based on knaves : **Jack Diamonds** – Hector, Prince of Troy.

Andrew Robson Esquire, himself a Devil incarnate, is widely regarded as being the finest Bridge player/teacher/writer in the world, having won the world Junior Championships in 1989, the British Gold Cup twice, and the silver medal in the World Individual.

I will pay my £10 to Lorna, one of Andrew's avid little groupie/helpers, and join a table of four sparring contenders.

Nineteen points, evenly split.

What the hell do I bid?

My hand will go up . . .

'An-drewwww!!!!'

5.30 p.m.   Thomas Martyn Foundation at the London Rowing Club

In 1647 a Thomas Martyn, gentleman, was buried in St Mary's Church, Putney.

Thomas had lived in a fine house there, Copt Hall, which had gardens extending down to the river, with its own private water steps and a landing stage.

Around 1630 he fell into the Thames one day, only to be rescued by local watermen.

No formal system of public education existed in Britain until the late 19th century, yet upon his death in 1684, Thomas Martyn, by will, appreciatively built and endowed a school for teaching, feeding and partly clothing twenty sons of watermen, who wore a uniform with coat, cap and girdle. The master was to receive £80 and was to be skilled in mathematics, so that presumably the rudiments of navigation might be taught.

This school, with 18 children, continued to exist and operate until 1911.

There is still a charity, of which I am a Governor, known today as the Thomas Martyn Foundation.

Our meeting this evening is to discuss the forthcoming Commemoration Service in St Mary's Church, to be attended by the young Foundationers (children of Watermen), parents and Governors.

We shall then discuss the subsequent reception that is to be held at the London Rowing Club, where Foundationers will each be presented with a cheque, seniors £125 and juniors £105; oh - and an orange.

Yes, an ORANGE!

This gift of an orange goes back to the days when oranges were a luxury seldom seen in the stalls in Putney or beyond.

In 1715 an Irish comedian, Thomas Doggett, founded a sculling race from London Bridge to Chelsea, a distance of four miles and four furlongs, with a prize of an orange red coat and silver badge, to celebrate the anniversary of the accession of the House of Hanover to the throne of England, The 'wager' has been rowed every year since 1715, and is claimed to be the oldest annual sporting event in the world! So – we will next discuss the invitations to this event that we shall be sending to the Master and Clerk of the Watermen's Company, the Bargemaster - and Dogget's Liverymen.

7.30 Royal Geographical Society

In 2003 I was elected to become a Fellow of the Royal Geographical Society.

The 'Geographical Society of London' was founded in 1830, as a dining club to promote the 'advancement of geographical science'.

The history of the Society in its earlier years was associated with 'colonial' exploration in Africa, the Indian subcontinent, the Polar regions and central Asia.

It has supported many notable explorers and expeditions, including those of Darwin, Livingston, and Stanley, Scott and Shackleton, Hunt and Hillary.

In 1911 the election as President of Earl Curzon, the former Viceroy of India, was significant to the Society.

The Society's President today is Michael Palin.

This evening there is to be a talk given to us by Mr Max Jones, entitled *Scott of the Antarctic: From Hero to Villain?*

I am looking forward to this very much indeed.

I shall enter the portals of the Society's physical and spiritual home at 1 Kensington Gore, London SW7 - one of the finest examples of 19th century architecture - walk into our impressive 750-seat hall and sink into my comfortable leather seat, mentally offering up my renewed thanks as I do so to its generous benefactor, Sir Christopher Ondaatje, whose name is enshrined in this lecture theatre.

'Please may I remind you to switch your mobile telephones back on at the end of the talk,' says a smiling Michael Palin, taking the chair to introduce this evening's speaker to us.

A hush rustles and settles over the room.

Max Jones takes the floor to engross us by unfolding and recounting the heroic story of the explorer Robert Falcon Scott's transition from owner of a Plymouth brewery, his promotion to become the Captain of *Discovery* and *Terra Nova*, his bickering with Shackleton, the battling against Amundsen, and his tragically perishing with the famed Captain Titus Oates and his other companions, frostbitten, snow-blinded, hungry and exhausted, on their fateful 800 mile return journey from the South Pole . . .

As I left the Royal Geographical Society's prestigious Kensington Gore establishment that evening, a century later, I felt reminded that it is still ever so good indeed to have been born British.

Mindful of our nation's great explorers, after nearly 80 years of knocking around this world of ours in various guises, I still see horizons to be discovered, peaks to be challenged, oceans to be crossed, and extraordinary people to be encountered on this amazing Earth.

Mine, certainly, has been a most enjoyable and wonderful life.

I do sincerely hope that in its eventual summing up, you will feel that yours, too, has been as good . . .

Grasp every opportunity that comes your way, *create* opportunities of your own and make them work for you – and it will be!

Good luck.

Brian Gilbart-Denham
Putney
Londinium
2011